SHUT UP

Stop Overthinking

Reduce Stress and Anxiety through Personal Development and Healthy Habits

Jennifer Stone

Introduction

"Life is too short to be sad."

You may have heard this very sensible advice voiced by your elders and many self-help experts.

It's true: life's too short to spend too much time worrying. After all, none of us can deny that certain life troubles make it difficult for happiness to settle into our lives.

Human lives are full of threatening challenges, setbacks and obstacles that can demoralise our spirits and seem so immovable that finding a way out seems impossible.

Not to mention change is an inevitable part of life. We cannot fight it nor can we find ways to cut lifes corners. No matter who you are or how much you try to hide from it, at some point in your life you will have to deal with change at some point in one form or the other. The main reason behind this is that we don't have any real control over our external environment, circumstances, people or their behaviours.

Since we have very little control over external change, we have to learn to accept what's coming our way rather than put energy into dwelling on it. That said, many problems we face are internal and can be a result of:

- *The doubts that can start to cripple our self-esteem*

- *The woes that don't exist, but continue to eat away at our happiness*

- *The thoughts in our minds that unnerve us*

- *The worries that fail to leave our consciousness*

Most of our problems exist even when they're not there. They live in our mind, consciousness, and sphere of thoughts.

If you haven't guessed it already, I am referring to the tendency to overthink, something many experts on the subject are now calling a "widely-spread epidemic" of sorts.

A study conducted by the University of Michigan discovered that around 73% of adults aged between 25-35 overthink, whilst in the same study, researchers also found that 52% of people aged 45-55 identify as overthinkers.

From these numbers, you can see that overthinking is one of the most pressing concerns we have to deal with today. Sadly, many of us don't address it seriously, and without realising becomes a part of our daily routines.

We often obsess over trivial matters and worry about problems that don't exist or have a lack of fundamental importance. That is how many of us go about dealing with our day to day thoughts, and because we have become accustomed to live our lives this way, many of us experience the following issues:

- *Anxiety that keeps us from feeling at ease*

- *Making mistakes in important tasks because we lack focus*

- *Missing many reasons to smile because we ponder over meaningless things*

- *Experiencing bodily pains that can drain us physically*

- *Obsessing over things and people that bring us little joy*

Overthinking can cause all this and then some, but unfortunately, we are often so busy obsessing over thoughts and problems that we often fail to recognise the negative consequences brought on by this tendency.

I am sure that you want to be happier, healthier, more self-assured, courageous, peaceful, focused, and optimistic in life.

I know that you want to live every day to its fullest and make the most of your time and energy. You want to smile more, maintain focus on important things, be with people who make you happy, engage in tasks that bring you joy, live in the moment, and invest your time and energy into things that truly matter to you.

For all of that to happen, you need to commit to self-betterment today. You need to vow to break free from the tendency to overanalyse thoughts, especially stressful ones!

It is best to take the slow and gradual approach towards this self-betterment, but you must stay true to the commitment. Once you make that vow, you need to start working on it dedicatedly, which is where this book comes in.

SHUT UP Stop Overthinking is a comprehensive and easy-to-follow guide that aims to show you how to stop overthinking for good, thus helping you overcome anxiety, experience reduced stress, and live a happier life.

The book aims to help you accomplish this goal by providing you with _actionable and proven techniques and strategies guaranteed to help you reclaim your life from overanalysing your thoughts._

The book begins by educating you about overthinking. From there, it walks you through the different types of unhealthy thought patterns and how overthinking sabotages your well-being, explaining numerous, practical and effective personal development tricks, and habits you can use to break free from the shackles of overthinking.

As you turn from one page to the next, you'll become more aware of why overthinking is a problem and learn ways to counteract it for good. By the time you get to the last page, you will have learned many helpful and practical strategies allowing you to reach a peaceful mind state.

Let's get started

Contents

Chapter 1: What is Overthinking

An anonymous quote reads:

*"**Overthinking:** the art of creating new problems out of the ones that never existed."*

This quote paints a very sad, but also very true picture. When we obsess over an idea or thought, we create more worries for ourselves, when we have no real cause for worry.

In reality, I think its safe to say that we all overthink at some point in our lives, and you know what? That's natural.

Most of the time it's the smallest events that often take up the most space in our minds. For example, we may spend time obsessing and coming up with scenarios of how a new interaction will go. We may fret about what our friend or partner meant when they texted back a short answer instead of a long message accompanied by emojis.

Worrying in these scenarios resonates with many of us, and as you can probably admit, we have all been in situations like these. With that said, you should understand that overthinking once in a while when necessary, is not harmful. However, when the practice becomes a regular part of your daily life, it gets embedded into your internal program and begins to make it very difficult for you to think rationally. No matter how hard you try, you just cannot shut your brain up and relax.

This chapter will help you get a more in-depth understanding of the problem and how it manifests.

What Does Obsessing Over a Thought Mean?

Overthinking refers to thinking way too much about a situation than it warrants. Instead of taking any meaningful action to resolve an issue, you begin stressing out over what has, or what may happen about an event. You overanalyse, fret over, repeat, and comment on the same thoughts repeatedly.

For instance, if you constantly thinking about whether you came across well or embarrassed yourself at your friend's party a few days ago and cannot stop your mind from obsessing over it, you are overthinking.

Similarly, if you find yourself wandering off in thought, overanalysing a situation that occurred in the day, thinking maybe, if you did it this way you'd have a better outcome, then you are over-scrutinising your thought processes, even though it doesn't change a thing.

When it comes to overthinking many people often associate it with mental health problems, such as anxiety and depression. Although this isn't always the case, many people experience varing levels of these issues, and all in all, it's quite difficult to say which occurs first when you overanalyse.

You may have anxiety that makes you overthink, and it is even possible that your habit of overanalysing things makes you susceptible to anxiety. This phenomenon is more like the "what came first: the chicken or the egg?" dilemma, a mystery that never gets solved.

Whether we first experience an emotional problem or an overthinking habit, the fact remains that the issue affects our mental health and emotional well-being. Whether you are walking, eating, driving, or anything else, a concern is always on your mind, brewing anxiety, not allowing you to let it go.

When looking at depression, being chained to a unstoppable thought that repeats the same issues can leave you feeling in a rut, many often feel consumed to the point that they find if difficult to find joy until its solved, which actually, in turn, sparks more thoughts on the same issue.

Some, especially those prone to overthinking, defend their habit by referring to it as "problem-solving" or "self-reflection." However, in reality, overthinking differs significantly from the two.

Let's discuss the differences between them

Problem-solving vs. Overthinking

Problem-solving consists of actively and rationally analysing a problematic, real situation.

When you think about solving a problem, you don't obsess over what went wrong. You know you're facing a particular problem or challenge and you try to solve it.

When comprehending the situation, you put on your thinking cap and start working towards finding a solution. Once you have identified possible resolutions, you choose an option and actively start working on it.

In contrast, when you overthink, you struggle to reach any tangible conclusion. You simply cannot stop your mind from racing and find yourself stuck in the middle of a convoluted maze of irritating and upsetting thoughts. As a result, you cannot settle on a workable conclusion or encourage yourself to take any action. All you can do is dwell on the issue.

Self-reflection vs. Overthinking

Self-reflection refers to reflecting on your thoughts and ideas to learn more about yourself as an individual, and gain broader perspectives on different ideas and situations.

Self-reflection is a purposeful practice that helps you gain deeper self-insight that allows you to identify your strengths, weaknesses, aspirations, ambitions, dreams, purpose, and vision in life.

At the end of any self-reflection session, you learn something new about yourself. At other times, you gain a profound understanding of an existing fact related to you, your existence, or an issue at hand. This realisation can enable better decisions to be made and steer your life in a more meaningful direction.

Opposed to this, overthinking keeps you from thinking peacefully, profoundly, and rationally about yourself. Instead of being purposeful, its primary characteristic is meaningless thinking that leads to nothing. You continue dwelling on how certain things failed to go as planned and continue worrying yourself for no good reason. You don't develop any understanding or insight into a situation, let alone yourself.

Overanalysing floods our minds with thought, which shows that unfortunately, overanalysing encourages us to focus on belaboring pointless things that end up being a waste of time. Even if you analyse your previous behavior and past experiences but don't learn anything from them, this even more clearly shows that your overthinking habit is for naught.

There are many different types of overthinking, but all of them boil down to two major categories. While we will discuss the other types of overthinking in the next chapter, let's explain their essence.

The Two Major Kinds of Overthinking

If you analyse the different thought processes related to overthinking, you will realise that they boil down to either *ruminating* or *obsessing over the future*.

Ruminating is the act of constantly worrying about your past and basing your present and future concerns on it.

When you're ruminating, your mind is full of a string of related, repetitive thoughts, or often just one thought that continues to play itself on repeat for hours, days, and sometimes even weeks.

While you may not want to feel that way, somehow, you cannot keep yourself from continuously thinking about the same worries. Thus, the same cycle of usually sad or even dark thoughts perpetuates itself incessantly in your mind, that can often make you feel stressed.

For instance, if you fumbled while giving a presentation in your team meeting and overheard a couple of participants laughing, you may overthink that you made a fool of yourself.

You may dwell on the worry for days, and because of it, you may not perform optimally in your job for quite some time.

The other type of overthinking involves over-scrutinising a future instance, but it works similarly to rumination. The primary difference is that here, you worry about something you anticipate happening.

Based on some setbacks that may have occurred in your life, you have a habit of imagining worst-case scenarios. Sometimes, the bad outcome you are apprehensive of may have a high probability of happening, but most of the time, your apprehensions are invalid.

For instance, if you haven't yet received your salary from your day job, you will probably start worrying about how you'll pay your rent and other dues for the month. This apprehension results from a concrete and actual event, and it is legitimate for you to worry about it. However, when you continue to over-scrutinise the situation without taking any meaningful action to make ends meet, you are overthinking without achieving any productive outcome.

Let's flip the script and look at another example to help you understand when you overthink pointlessly about situations, that have low odds of happening.

If you've been paying your bills on time every month, have received your salary, and have all your finances under control but still worry about failing to manage everything or going bankrupt, you're overthinking.

In this situation, the odds of that happening aren't too high, but you cannot keep yourself from stressing about it.

Whether you're dwelling on the past or stressing about a future concern, both types of worries cause a racing mind state:

What is a Racing State of Mind?

Think back to a time when you were thinking extremely rapidly. Amp up that feeling by many notches and make it persistent without pauses between thoughts. That is what it feels like to have racing thoughts. When you have racing thoughts on repeat, you experience a racing state of mind.

Racing thoughts go beyond thinking fast. They are an ongoing succession of thoughts that continue unlimited and are very difficult to silence. They tend to take over your functional consciousness, often jumping out of control to the extent that they tend to sabotage your daily life. Those who experience racing thoughts usually complain of having sleep problems too.

Having racing thoughts is one of the first symptoms of overthinking. You can easily identify this symptom in yourself because you tend to speak rapidly and leap from one branch of thought to another, just like a monkey in the jungle. Because of this apt comparison, you'll also often hear a racing state of mind called the "monkey state of mind." Moreover, because these feelings tend to manifest outwardly, many people also refer to this state as a "flight of ideas."

Hence, a flight of ideas and racing thoughts are more like two sides of one coin. They usually revolve around certain rhythms and resemble a broken, soundless record because when you pick up a certain idea or worry, you allow it to play on repeat in your mind.

Whether you're a ruminator or prone to fretting too much about future concerns, the reality is, the tendency isn't constructive at all. You do not achieve any positive outcomes from the entire process; it only takes a toll on your sanity. I will elaborate on the harms of overthinking in a later chapter to ensure you become more stimulated to curb this practice.

For now, let us move on to the different types of negative and overthinking thoughts that keep you from feeling focused, relaxed, and centered.

Chapter 2: Understanding The Different Kinds of Overthinking

An anonymous quote reads:

"There is nothing in the world that can trouble you as much as your own thoughts."

Besides yourself, everything else in the world is beyond your control. Only you have control over your thoughts, your attitude, and your actions. To be happy, you need to work on all the elements within your control.

Since our thoughts influence our attitudes and actions, it is important to start working on them first. When you let an upsetting thought run astray, it starts spewing venom in your mind.

One negative thought leads to another, and before you realise it, there is a storm of negativity in your mind. When you overthink, you give life to similar thoughts in your head, thoughts that will only create more problems and make your life very difficult.

To help yourself get over the problem successfully, the first thing you should do is gain insight into the different types of overthinking. When you have a complete comprehension of a problem, you can take the right measures to overcome it for good. The same applies to overthinking.

This chapter will walk you through the many types of overthinking, helping you understand how you overthink and how it affects your life.

1: Going Overboard with Abstractions

This happens when you go completely overboard with abstractions to the extent that they feel completely alienated from reality.

In problem-solving, abstractions refer to going through a problem as a whole instead of being specific. You analyse the problem at hand, eliminate the extra details, and simplify it to find a solution with ease.

Although this approach can help you solve the trickiest of problems, it turns into overthinking when you keep obsessing over an issue.

For instance, suppose you're only mulling over how and why you haven't gotten your big break in acting and are still a struggling actor. In that case, you fixate on the thought to the extent that you start fussing over the issue and upsetting yourself in the process. You don't get anything done to overcome the problem; you only become engulfed in more worries.

Going overboard with abstraction also manifests as another issue: focusing on the complexity of an issue.

Focusing on the complexity of an issue usually happens when you think about too many associated factors without factoring in their importance to the issue.

For instance, if you are planning on attending a party with your partner where you'll meet their parents, you may start worrying about the following:

- If you will present yourself in a positive way

- Whether you will look or be good enough

- How the parents will greet you and what you'll talk about

- Whether they will like you

Instead of just being yourself, you start obsessing over every little aspect of the issue, making mountains out of molehills. This type of overthinking [usually] takes away your attention from what truly matters and onto many trivial factors.

Because you cannot stop fussing about the tiny details, you often turn every little problem into a complicated one.

2: Avoiding the Problem

This overthinking strain happens when you avoid the real problem using the excuse of the decision-making process as being too complicated.

Understandably, making some decisions is not straightforward; it involves many steps, strategies, and techniques. However, if you avoid accepting and facing a problem with this excuse, you are prone to stressing over the issue and becoming unable to think clearly in the process.

For example, you may have to decide whether you will accept a job offer that requires you to relocate. However, since the thought of making that move is overwhelming for you, you keep postponing the issue and the decisions because you are scared of even considering the idea of packing and leaving to another place.

When you avoid an actual matter, it keeps you from reaching a productive conclusion and makes you continue obsessing over matters that you can solve with ease. This only exacerbates the issue and strains your mind with many tensions.

When your thoughts are spiraling out of control and find you're avoiding the problem, there are a few common excuses and approaches that my be exacerbating the problem:

2a: *Exercising cold logic*

Logic is an efficient tool that helps you analyse situations to reach a workable decision. However, logic is not the ultimate solution to every decision. Some decisions require you to think and act emotionally, not just logically.

In such situations, if you're using logic to avoid thinking emotionally, you are using cold logic. It won't get you any viable outcome and will only exhaust you emotionally in the end.

You revert to logic only because you are scared of embracing your emotions. While you do seem to handle the situation on the surface, deep down, you are frustrated and overwhelmed because you know you are not putting your best foot down.

For instance, you may realise that you love someone but are also afraid of accepting your feelings for them. When that person confesses their love for you, you refuse to accept that you feel the same way because you afraid of getting hurt because your previous relationships did not go too well. Chances are you may get too scared of getting hurt that you get cold feet and start distancing yourself from them. While you need to think emotionally in this matter, you make your decision using cold logic.

The problem in such situations is that even though you seem to convince yourself or the others involved in the decision, you don't feel satisfied. Instead, you keep ruminating over it and become flooded with worry.

2b: Exercising unnecessary emotional reasoning

This is the opposite of applying cold logic.

This type of avoidance and negative thought process makes you draw emotion-based conclusions. Just because you feel something, you believe it to be true even if there is no solid evidence justifying your thoughts, ideas, or decisions besides those feelings.

Perhaps you had plans for dinner with your best friend, but they canceled last minute because they urgently had to see their ailing father. While you are certain they aren't lying, you start overthinking it. You obsess over the idea that they may not want to spend time with you and don't wish to stay friends. Before you realise it, stress has flooded your mind and body.

It is important and even healthy to feel emotions strongly and tune into your gut feeling to make an informed decision. However, not every decision should be based entirely on your emotions, especially flimsy ones not backed by sound reasoning.

2c: *Making irrelevant decisions*

This is when you make an utterly irrelevant decision that's opposed to what you ought to be thinking and working on, only to avoid the actual issue.

Perhaps you have to arrange a baby shower for your friend but cannot get started with it because you keep worrying about if everything will go to plan. The worry overwhelms you so much that you decide to postpone the organising in favor of catching up with the latest episode of the series you've been watching.

This decision is not what you need to make for the situation at hand, but you make it only to avoid thinking and working on the actual issue.

Making irrelevant decisions wastes your time, energy, money, and other resources. Moreover, it aggravates the matter since the actual problem still exists. You chose to ignore it by making another irrelevant decision and end up increasing your worries.

2d: *Making a Premature Decision*

Many key decisions demand that you mull them over deeply. However, many others do not demand such profound contemplation.

If you are prone to overthinking, you probably spend a lot of your resources and time avoiding the issue by over-analysing and making a decision that is not necessary right now—or even ever. We call this making a premature decision, and usually, you do so to avoid thinking about the problems at hand.

Perhaps you're dating someone, and the adrenaline rush you get when you're around them convinces you that they're the one, so you make rash decisions to speed up the relationship, e.g. you decide to move in with them, only to realise later that you should have gotten to know each other better.

Later, when you realise that you made a premature decision in a rush, you consider rectifying it by speaking to your partner, which is likely to relationship strife.

That is just one example of making a premature decision. Every time you make a hasty decision, you create more trouble for yourself which can burden you and others.

3: Catastrophising

Also called 'magnification,' catastrophising involves obsessing over a problem to the extent that you blow it out of proportion. The problem usually does not exist, but you over-scrutinise the matter so strangely so soon, you have many worrisome problems.

For instance, let's imagine your partner says they need some time to themselves because they need to get a few things done. Because your first reaction is to approach the information negatively, you automatically think there is an issue in the relationship and they don't love you anymore.

Catastrophising makes you think of the worst-case scenarios in every situation. You don't even pause to think of any other outcome because you are sure only terrible things will happen.

Catastrophising can manifest in various, covert ways:

3a: Discounting the positives of a situation

Most of those prone to catastrophising and obsessing over matters also discount any positives associated with the situation.

Also known as 'minimising,' this strain of overthinking keeps you from considering what's positive about a situation. Even if something good happens to you, you minimise it to the point that it seems barely noticeable.

Doing this gives you more room to overthink what's negative about a situation. In essence, when you discount what's positive, you cannot help but overthink, which is why you struggle to accept positivity.

For instance, if you score a good grade in an exam, you think you just got lucky and that the result has nothing to do with all the late-night studying you did. If your friend tells you that they like spending time with you and enjoys your company, you just think they're trying to be nice to you, and start to think of all your weaknesses that they may soon discover.

3b: Practicing over-optimisation

When you focus on tweaking the minor details associated with a situation and overlook the bigger picture in the process, you are over-optimising. The bigger problem is likely to be something that deserves your actual time and attention. However, since it feels overwhelming, you find it easier to mull over the minute details and fuss about them instead of doing the needful.

Perhaps you have to give a keynote speech at a seminar, but the mere idea of it scares you, especially since you feel you aren't good at public speaking. Thus, instead of preparing your speech, you decide to go shopping to buy something to wear to the seminar. Your attire shouldn't be your primary focus area, but you choose to overlook what's important because thinking about it stresses you out.

3c: Experiencing Analysis Paralysis

Analysing a situation is a very effective decision-making tool. It allows you to break a problem into its basic components, assess each of them in detail, and then reach a conclusion. However, if you are susceptible to obsessing over matters, you probably often struggle with analysis paralysis.

Analysis paralysis occurs when you over-scrutinise an issue to the extent that you become flooded with myriads of problems and struggle to make any decision at all.

You spend so much time and energy worrying about irrelevant details, hoping to make the perfect decision, that you end up feeling overwhelmed and unable to make any decision at all. Your mind fails to function rationally and optimally because you have overburdened it with unnecessary details.

Analysis paralysis keeps you from making informed and rational decisions and taking a step forward in the right direction. It causes you to overstress matters that don't deserve your attention, preventing you from taking any meaningful action.

3d: Struggling with the fear of failure

Nobody likes to go through failure. It hurts and demotivates you from pursuing your goals. However, failure is a stepping stone to success. If you perceive it as something positive, you can use it constructively to your advantage and work your way up the success ladder, but only if you have a positive attitude towards it.

If you overthink, the chances are high that you are scared of failing in any aspect of life. You fear it to the degree that you stop taking risks and experimenting in life. You only know how to play safe because you feel that no other option exists. You often go overboard with avoiding the fear of failure and keep yourself from being happy.

Deep down, you're well aware of your fears and insecurities, but instead of facing them, you allow them to eat away at your joy.

Perhaps you have always wanted to start a business you feel passionate about. However, since you saw your dad struggle with establishing his business, you fear you won't be good at it and will experience failure and difficulties. This fear keeps you from pursuing your passion, and instead, you're stuck in a 9 to 5 job you dislike.

3e: Carrying out fortune telling

Fortune telling involves predicting bad outcomes in the foreseeable future. This tendency keeps you from seeing the future optimistically; it also makes you see everything in a negative light. Since you have a skewed attitude, you tend to act negatively, inviting bigger problems and issues.

For instance, you panic before a job interview because you overthink your performance. You keep fretting about it, imagining worst-case scenarios, lose your cool, and as a result, perform poorly. You hold onto that bad outcome and perceive it as proof of your correct judgment, which isn't true.

In reality, it's your negative thought process that draws unpleasant experiences towards you, that keeps you from being happy. However, you fail to comprehend that, which is why you continue to overthink, practice fortune-telling, and expect to attract negative outcomes.

4: Mind Reading

Mind reading involves assuming you know exactly how and what someone else is thinking and are positive that it reflects negatively on you.

For example, if you see someone glancing at you, you assume they're thinking negatively about you or making fun of you in their mind. If you're talking, but your friend has eyes for her phone instead of looking at you, you may think they're not interested in what you have to say and that you're boring them.

Since you are prone to thinking negatively about everything and blaming yourself for every problem you experience, you may assume every situation revolves around you. No matter what situation, you find something negative about it and use it to target and blame yourself. You are likely to hold onto these thoughts, and you may fixate on them for days, weeks and even months, blowing them out of proportion.

5: Personalisation

Personalisation happens when you make up certain things about yourself when they are unrelated to you.

Blaming yourself for things beyond your control, taking things very personally even though they are not directed at you or intended to hurt you, and thinking you are the root cause of everything negative are all examples of personalisation in practice.

For example, you may blame yourself for your parents' divorce due to your behaviour as a child. If a colleague asks you to hand them a file without smiling at you, you think they're being rude to you. Overall, when you personalise, every problem centers on you, and you find it difficult to stop yourself from incessantly worrying about it.

You may practice all these types of overthinking or habitually practice any one or two more often. Either way, you habitually overanalyse things which is certainly not a healthy practice to nurture.

With what we've learned so far, it is possible that you might be wondering; "Just how bad can it get?". Lucky for you, the next chapter will help you discover and appreciate the need to do something by understanding how overthinking causes stress and anxiety.

Chapter 3: How Overthinking Leads to Stress and Anxiety

An English proverb once said:

> *"Worrying is like sitting in a rocking chair. It gives you something to do, but it doesn't get you anywhere."*

When you overthink, you may contemplate your thoughts for days, weeks, and even months, but you are likely to get nowhere because you are not doing anything substantial. Overthinking never gets you anywhere: it never has and never will, which is why it's so unfortunate that many of us are susceptible to it and allow it to wreak havoc in our lives.

While overthinking isn't a "real" medical phenomenon, research shows that it adversely influences your mental and emotional well-being. It makes you rehash the past, focus on the negatives of a situation, dwell on upsetting experiences, and fret about the future.

Ashley Carroll is a certified psychologist who works with the Parkland Memorial Hospital. She notes that whenever we fixate on particular negative thoughts, they eventually snowball into more convoluted and upsetting ones. The thoughts then turn into beliefs that affect our attitudes, actions, and decisions.

If you start to think this way every day, it becomes your go-to thought process and begins to influence your daily life. Carroll strongly believes—and has seen in her patients—that overthinking starts to impair our optimal daily functioning.

When you're a chronic overthinker, you are likely to struggle with sleeping easily and comfortably at night. You may also lose your appetite because you often get lost in your thoughts. Sometimes, you may find yourself eating more than you need, but even then, you are likely to be unaware of the taste of the food because you are inattentive to the practice.

Let's take a closer look at how overthinking can transform into stress, anxiety, and even depression, and how it may sabotage your well-being.

How Overthinking Can Lead To Stress, Anxiety, And Depression

Overthinking has a close bond with emotional disorders such as anxiety, depression, and stress. Let us explore these aspects one by one.

How overthinking causes anxiety

As we know, it is very natural to worry about upsetting situations in life, especially when confronted with something unexpected.

However, when you continue to experience panicky, anxious, and fearful thoughts in situations that aren't debilitating, it is almost always followed by a constant and nagging worry which in some instances can cause panic attacks. If you are now reflecting on how you approach unforeseen situations, and feel as though panic often follows closely, you may have an anxiety disorder.

Having a chronic anxiety disorder affects your ability to function optimally and maintain healthy relationships in life. According to Our World in Data, 2018, 264 million adults around the globe had anxiety and of these, 179 million were female (63%) and 105 million were male (37%).

Anxiety disorders develop when you worry about future events and outcomes. For example, when you continue stressing over how you may perform in your job interview, whether you will pass an exam, if you'll will get along well with your partner's parents, and similar worries repeatedly, you start to overthink.

When vicious thoughts play in a loop and continue to upset you, anxiety paves the way for overthinking. That said, this can also happen the other way around.

If you constantly analyse an idea and start to worry about the future and any other outcome associated with it, you become anxious. You may begin to catastrophise, foresee negative outcomes, discount the positives, and focus only on the negatives. Incessantly fretting about the future soon drives you towards anxiety. When this practice becomes a regular part of your routine life, it can make you prone to anxiety disorders.

How overthinking causes depression

There are times in our life when we feel sad, discouraged, and hopeless. It is alright to feel that way occasionally when you've had a bad day or when problems come at you, one after another.

That said, if such feelings drown you every day and persist for more than two weeks, it could be a sign that you're struggling with depression.

Although each person may experience different indications of depression, there are a few commonly occurring symptoms; discouragement, hopelessness, sadness, low energy levels, bouts of anger, losing interest in activities you earlier found interesting and feeling overwhelmed by personal interactions and daily tasks.

We discussed how one of the major types of overthinking is ruminating on your memories; repeatedly rehashing the painful past and traumatic events of your life.

Depression can intensify the way you see things, more specifically focusing on the negative. Hence, when you fixate on your troubling past, you may feel woeful and dejected. Likewise, depression can push you to obsession. Worries related to an emotionally draining event may be constantly present in your mind, causing you to play it on repeat, day in and day out.

Whether depression leads to overanalysing or the other way around, the truth is that the two only exacerbate the problem by worsening your mental health.

How overthinking causes stress

Many of us often confuse stress with anxiety, but the two are very different. Stress is your body's natural and normal response to anything you perceive as challenging and pressurising.

For example, if you are going through a breakup or divorce you are likely to feel stressed. You may also feel frustrated when you discover that your boss has placed you in charge of a large team. As a result, when threatening situations present themselves, many of us often respond with stress, especially when they're unexpected.

Whenever you encounter a challenging situation, your brain activates the stress response—or the fight, flight, or freeze response. Once this response is active, our bodies experience a series of physiological changes like rapid heartbeat, increased blood flow to the limbs and muscle tightening.

These changes can prepare you to cope with a stressful situation in 3 ways, 1) facing it, 2) fleeing from it, or 3) freezing. These changes happen because the body triggers the release of stress hormones, cortisol and adrenaline.

Stresses—and the bodily changes it causes—usually fade away when a stressful situation passes. However, suffering from anxiety means that this change may persist for long periods as its often a rooted problem.

Moreover, anxiety mainly encompasses worrisome thoughts related to the future, whereas stress can relate to thoughts about the past, present, or future.

While stress usually goes away when your stressors reduce, chronic stress tends to linger on for a little too long than we would like. Chronic stress is when all the signs and symptoms of stress become heightened and persist for quite some time.

Like anxiety and depression, stress and overthinking have a direct relationship and are interdependent.

When you obsess over different setbacks, thoughts, and situations, it tends to exhaust you emotionally, mentally, and physically. For example, if you cannot stop fretting about submitting 100 orders in two days, or how failing find a job in time may affect your financial position, your overthinking leads to stress. Because of it, you may find yourself experiencing chronic headaches, neck, shoulder, or back pain.

Likewise, stress may trigger your tendency to obsess over certain thoughts too. For instance, if, out of the blue, your boss announces that you, not your colleague, will present the new project to the organisation's Board of Directors, and the meeting is due in half an hour, you are likely to find yourself pacing around the room in stress.

You may worry about maintaining your calm during the presentation, how you will remember all the points since you hadn't prepared like your colleague had, and whether you will leave a good impression on your superiors. You start to over-scrutinise all these concerns and obsess on them for hours. That's an example of how stress transforms into overthinking.

Everything we have discussed so far in this chapter should clarify the inter-relatedness of these issues. Let's delve a bit deeper and talk more about how they affect the quality of your life.

How Overthinking, Stress, Anxiety, and Depression Decrease your General Well-being

Overthinking and the stress, anxiety, and depression it causes can affect your general well-being in the following ways:

1: Lack of focus on the present moment

Overthinking keeps you busy with rehashing the past or panicking about the future. When you're overthinking, there is usually no in between, which means you completely disregard your present.

You need to understand that we all live in the present moment. Thus, it's vital that you mentally and physically anchor yourself to the moment. When you're overthinking, you cannot do that because you lack control over your urges to worry about the past or fret about the future.

This habitual tendency presents the following problems:

- You lack focus on the tasks at hand. For example, if you're watering your plants, you may also be circling negative thoughts about your relationship.

- Failing to concentrate on your tasks, means that you may struggle to do them attentively, making more errors along the way. You may find yourself reading the same sentence repeatedly as you aren't paying sole attention to the task at hand.

- You may find you never feel grounded to the present moment, nor experience it fully. Because of lurking in the past or future, you can only imagine experiencing the joy of living in the present moment.

This lack of focus and involvement in the present moment brings forth many other problems. However, being aware that you are doing it is the first step to taking action.

2: You lack enjoyment in your tasks

When you're inattentively doing something, its hard to get full enjoyment out of it. It is quite probable that the lack of contentment and joy stems from not being grounded and involved in your tasks. You may be reading your favorite book or watching a video, but since you fail to concentrate on the task and invest yourself in it, you don't enjoy it as much as you should.

Lacking interest and excitement in the things you do makes them monotonous. If you have ever complained of frequently not being able to find joy in things you do, the root cause of it is likely to be mindlessness.

3: You become less productive

We all have some days when we don't feel like doing anything. On such days, we usually have to drag ourselves to work and find it hard to complete our tasks, which usually leads us to carrying a negative energy throughout the day.

You are well aware of the deliverables you need to submit and the deadlines you have to meet. When there is mounting pressure to complete your high-priority tasks, some of us find it difficult to force ourselves to do so because we fixate on negative outcomes, this avoids the real problem, leading to abstraction; never thinking about the important tasks that matter.

Slowly, over time your habit of overanalysing worries cripples your productivity, and you may start performing poorly, and your obsession with concerns can seriously begin to affect your professional endeavors.

4: Suffering with Insomnia

When you become vulnerable to overthinking, sleepless nights of tossing and turning (and sometimes sweating) become a regular occurrence. Naturally, when all you can think about are your troubles, your mind continues to race when it should be relaxing and refreshing.

When its time to rest and relax your mind, you realise that somehow your mind just does not shut up. It is quite natural to lose your sleep in such situations where you don't know what to do, because you lack control over your thoughts.

5: You become irritable and experience mood swings

Overthinking is a very emotionally taxing experience. Twisted thoughts can weigh you down. Feeling as though you may need to isolate yourself from others, as sharing your feelings and thoughts with those around you is a task you wish not to delve in, and more often than not, results in emotions being bottled up.

However, since you are not releasing your emotions, fears, and insecurities through positive means, they build up inside you, and the storm keeps raging, which often projects on others.

Those who overthink are prone to anger management issues and mood swings. They may be subdued at one point but can become quite fiery and agitated the next.

6: Strained relationships with loved ones

Relationships thrive when there is love, care, trust, and sincerity from both ends. That becomes quite difficult to achieve when one of the involved parties gets victimised by overthinking.

If you over-scrutinise your thoughts and life situations, you may notice that you usually focus on the negatives and make every situation about you, that too, in a negative manner. If your partner is upset, you worry about whether they're angry that you keep unhelpfully questioning them on things that aren't related to what they might be stressing over.

This unsupportive behavior creates rifts in the relationships. These rifts grow stronger when you struggle to be available for your loved ones, particularly emotionally. Isolating yourself can weaken these relationships as you may begin to lack commitment to each other.

7: Declining mental and physical health

All the issues discussed above can negatively impact your mental and physical health. Naturally, when you feel demotivated, frustrated, vent your anger on others, feel as though you lose interest and focus in things you do, it decreases your mental well-being.

These emotional conditions such as stress, anxiety, and depression can sometimes manifest as chronic headaches and body pains, meaning that you may be more susceptible to having low energy levels due to the lack of sufficient rest. Unfortunately, we have all been victims of times like these.

Eventually, especially when they go unaddressed, such instances can lead to a sedentary lifestyle where being glued to the couch or staying locked in our room becomes second nature, causing a rut that adversely affects our well-being.

These issues that play out in our lives, one after another, or at the same time, can make life incredibly intense and stressful.

Deep down, I know you are tired of living for what at times can feel like a repetitive life. You know you deserve to be happy and content. You aspire to pursue activities that excite you and set goals that infuse your life with meaning. You want that and more, but somehow, your worries and tensions keep you from following through and achieving your wishes. Your wishes only stay as your heart's deepest desires that you feel as though may never be fulfilled.

You know what? That is where you are wrong.

- *You can face your fears, insecurities and worries head on*

- *You can let go of your continuous loop of repetitive, draining thoughts*

- *You can change your unhealthy beliefs into healthy ones for good*

- *You can be happy. You can be healthy. You can be peaceful. You can be prosperous.*

- *Whatever you wish for can be yours*

"How can all this happen?," you may wonder.

Well, as mentioned earlier, your thoughts are in your control. Your thoughts and everything related to your life are in your reach. You can be happy because you deserve it, and you have the power to change your life for the better. You can do it!

Now:

Please don't assume that this implies you should blame yourself for feeling that way; you should not. It only means that you need to get back on track and train your brain to stop thinking negatively and bothering yourself with things that don't exist and, in that case, are substantial enough to matter.

Doing that may seem like a very daunting task to you right now, but the reality is that it isn't all that complicated. It is doable, and you can achieve it. You have unlimited potential, a lot more than what you give yourself credit for, and it is high time you accept and utilise it the right way. And yes, I know that even though it is beneficial for you, doing so can seem tough at the start. This book seeks to make this process a bit easier for you. I want you to reclaim your life, be happy and healthy.

Let us move on to making that happen from the next chapter onwards, where we shall discuss personal development techniques, strategies, and habits that help you save yourself from the harms of overthinking for good.

Chapter 4: Understand Your Overthinking Symptoms

Irish playwrite George Bernard Shaw:

"People become attached to their burdens sometimes more than the burdens are attached to them."

Your burdens are not clinging to you as much you are clinging to them. When you stop thinking about a worry, trust me when I say that it will stop bothering you too. Worries only grow stronger and bigger when you cling to them.

Whatever you hold on to a worry, emotionally or physically, you think, and when you think about something repeatedly, it becomes a part of your thought process. It starts to shape your belief systems in the same manner, and soon, you have many similar beliefs and thoughts that affect you in a certain way.

Since we are talking about overthinking here, we can safely assume that when you overthink, because you're overthinking negative things, you nurture unhealthy beliefs and thought-patterns that add to your burdens.

Understandably, letting go of this habit is not easy, but trust me, if you take baby steps consistently, you can do it. Let us start this process by helping you become better aware of the different signs of overthinking.

When we are prone to behaving a certain way, we do not consciously pay attention to every step of the process. However, when it comes to treating the problem, we need to be attentive because that's the only viable way to solve an issue.

Signs and Symptoms Of Overthinking

Let discuss the different signs and symptoms of overthinking:

1: You don't focus on finding solutions

It's good to think deeply about your life and all the problems that affect you. However, if you're thinking without focusing on identifying a solution, you are only overthinking.

Let's take an instance where you hear about a storm approaching your area on the weather forecast.

Your sane mind may think to protect any lightweight furniture that might get damaged from the storm. On the other hand, when you overthink, you are likely to start thinking about how the storm will aggravate the problems in life and how you are sure it will damage your house in the process. Such thoughts cloud your rational state of mind, making it impossible for you to think creatively and develop viable solutions to issues.

2: Repetitive thoughts haunt you

You contemplate over one thing repeatedly without any limit on the time to worry about it.

For example, if you had a conversation with your friend that had a somewhat bitter flavor to it, you may replay it in your head like a broken record, fixating on the painful parts more.

If you have certain thoughts that never leave your mind, or if you allow specific negative experiences to haunt you, this may be a sign youre prone to overthinking.

3: You admire people who complete tasks

You want to do things that excite you. Perhaps you have a college assignment to complete or a new education target to pursue. You have aspirations but somehow lack the courage and willingness to fulfill them.

Since you cannot achieve them, you look for people working on the same or similar aspirations and aspire to be more like them, but that is where you stop: admiration.

You want to be like your friend who reads a book every day, or like your cousin who exercises regularly, but somehow you cannot do that because your thoughts never give you a chance to take forward-moving action.

4: You think about the WHY in everything

While it is important to figure out why you want to set and achieve a goal, if you find yourself asking yourself too many 'WHYs' associated with everything, you have a problem that you need to start working on immediately.

You may feel as though everything is intriguing, and you must get to the bottom of it, not because it matters to you but because you have a habit of picking out minor details and obsessing over them.

5: You ignore your gut instincts

According to psychologist Dr. Helen Odessky, ignoring your gut instinct is often a sign of being an over-thinker. All of us have a gut instinct, our intuitive voice that we tune into every time we have a critical or even simple decision to make.

If you ignore that and make a massive list of pros and cons to decide something, but even then, you don't make a decision, the chances are high that you overanalyse things a lot.

According to research published in The Proceedings of the National Academy of Sciences, participants who made a decision based on their instinct alone ended up making the right call a whopping 90% of the time, as opposed to those who analysed the issue logically.

When you disregard your gut feeling, you take it upon yourself to overanalyse the situation. Even while and after doing that, you never feel satisfied; you keep thinking about things for far too long.

6: You have the same conversations with people

If something bothers us, we may run it by some trustworthy loved ones. You probably do the same every time you have a big work-related project coming up, an important life transition, or any other substantial decision you have to make.

When we overthink, we repeatedly run the same ideas in our minds. Every time we analyse things, we frequently run the same ideas by our friends to discuss our points with them, which is usually another sign of overthinking.

If your loved ones tell you that you keep bringing up the same issue, or that they need a break from your habit of fussing about things, it means you have a severe overthinking problem that you need to address.

7: You need every piece of information to make a decision

Decision-making is not a very straightforward task, especially when you need to make important and big decisions. You have lots of information to scrutinise and assess before making the final call.

That said, there is a difference between getting your hands on ample information and going overboard with finding every piece of information there exists about a certain aspect.

If you focus on gathering every piece of conceivable information when making up your mind about something, but still don't feel convinced enough to make a choice, you are a victim of overthinking.

You look up the idea online, question your loved ones, ask your friends for suggestions, read books and articles, carry out your analysis, but still end up not deciding at all.

8: You ask yourself too many 'what if' questions

If every time you think of making a choice, you think up a bunch of never-ending 'what ifs' followed by imagining the worst-case scenario, or something that's a stretch from reality, you're a victim of overanalysing things.

Asking yourself too many 'what if' questions when making a decision is a classic sign of being an over-thinker. Since you are prone to thinking negatively, you cannot help but imagine what would happen if things go south. The instant you contemplate that aspect, your negative thoughts sprawl everywhere, growing their roots deeper in your mind.

9: You think of things you shouldn't have said or could have said better

Do you often find yourself replaying different conversations you had with people long after you have had them, worrying about the things you should or should not have said or could have said in a better manner? If so, you are prone to overthinking.

For you, it is customary to play out your daily events in your head. While you may carry out this practice with the hopes of learning from the experience, you may find yourself fixating on different thoughts and panicking as a result.

See, it is easy to get pulled into ruminative thinking, but understand that the past is just that: the past!

When we cannot go back in time and change things, stressing over the past is wasted energy. The only time that matters is the present, and you can be happy right now if you're committed to it.

10: *You get panic attacks often*

Panic attacks are brief episodes of heightened anxiety that produce intense physical feelings of fear and insecurity.

When you experience a panic attack, your heartbeat becomes rapid, your breath becomes short and fast, you tremble and feel dizzy, and you may also have muscle tension in the body.

Often, the symptoms resemble those of a heart attack, which can make it confusing. However, panic attacks are short-lived and usually end after some time. That said, they can be very exhausting, leaving you feeling drained and chaotic.

While the problem can have other root causes, heightened anxiety and overthinking are usually to blame.

11: *You think nobody understands you*

We are all individuals who think differently. With that said, we find people who understand us and support us in our good and bad times; with time, we become friends and feel close to them. Whenever we have a problem at hand, we run off to those friends for comfort and guidance because we know they will understand us.

However, this is not the case when you become a chronic overthinker. Your negative, twisted thoughts consume your energy to the extent that you find it hard to explain yourself to anyone.

While you want to share your feelings with your loved ones, you assume that they won't understand you. You may think people will make fun of you, not comprehend your feelings, and avoid you. Because of this, you stop pouring your heart out to loved ones, often feeling alone as a result.

Action step: Analyse yourself

Buy a journal dedicated to everything you'll learn from this book and keep it with you at all times. It is best to get a small, pocket-sized notebook that you can easily carry and take out to jot down points when needed.

Reflect on the signs of overthinking as deeply as possible and look for those cues in your behavior. If you find yourself deferring a task and missing a deadline, put that down in your journal. If you run conversations in your head repeatedly, note that down as well.

Copy the following table into your journal so you can record the time, date, situation, frequency, and intensity of the symptom. This way, you will note if you have a headache four times a week with an intensity of 7/10, or that you ignore your gut instincts each time you have to make a decision.

Symptom	Time	Date	Situation of Occurrence	Intensity (Out of 10)	Frequency (Number of Times a Day/Week)

Besides self-observation, you can ask a trustworthy friend to observe you too to help you eliminate as much bias as possible from the equation.

We tend to be biased towards ourselves at times and may ignore some signs. You may be putting off your tasks frequently but be ignorant of this issue instead of accepting it as a symptom of your overthinking habit.

However, if you have an honest and dependable friend observing you, they can give you their honest input that will help you grow. This support can allow you to become more self-aware of your weaknesses, enabling you to identify and improve them.

Once you become aware of how you overthink and the different ways an overthinking habit manifests, you will begin to understand your thought processes. This sense of awareness will empower and motivate you to overcome different kinds of stresses and constraints.

The next step is to start working on improving the problem. Doing that requires courage, strength, and commitment. The good news is that you have all of that locked up within you.

- *If it weren't for courage, you would not be here reading this book.*

- *If you weren't strong, you would not analyse yourself when you overthink, even though it is a daunting task.*

- *If you did not truly want to be happy, you wouldn't be making a concious effort to help yourself.*

You want to improve and are ready to do so, and with this guide by your side, there is nothing that can stop you from making that happen.

Now, move forward with me to discuss the different actionable self-help strategies you can start implementing now to improve your life. Now, lets embark on a new journey that invites happiness and peace your way.

Chapter 5: Set an Intention and Commit to the Cause

Lao Tzu once said:

"Do the difficult things while they are easy and do the great things while they are small. A journey of a thousand miles must begin with a single step."

Every journey you embark on in life begins with a single step. You have to replicate those steps, introduce different styles and sizes, and continue walking until you reach your final destination. This strategy applies to breaking your habit of overthinking as well.

To get started with the journey, you need to take the first step forward, which requires you to set an intention to commit yourself to the cause and dedicatedly follow through.

Why You Should Set an Intention and Commit Yourself to Your Goal

Observing yourself, especially when you overthink, gives insight into how and when you overthink. However, that does not amount to an open acceptance of the problem, nor does it show your intention to resolve the problem.

If you're to overcome any issue in your life, the crucial first step is openly acknowledging and accepting it, so that you know you have a problem to tackle. After that, you need to set a clear intention to work on it, understanding very well what you will be working towards achieving. Then, remind yourself of your goal time and again, ensuring you become engaged in it.

Day in and day out, when you think of what you have to do and how it adds value to your life, especially when you break it down to smaller goals, you automatically become excited about it. You see yourself achieving little milestones, and you become more invested in the process.

In a matter of weeks, you will see yourself breaking free of your vicious thoughts and restoring peace and sanity to your life.

All of this will happen, and you will reclaim your life, but it has to start with the first step.

1: Acknowledge your problem

Have you ever been through a time when you kept coughing and sneezing like crazy but kept denying that you had allergies, or a time when you kept hiding your tooth pains so that you didn't have to see a dentist?

Eventually, you had to accept your problem and get it treated. This is because the more you ignore your pain or allergies, the more the problem worsens.

This is what's happening to you right now, in terms of your tendency to overanalyse things. You may have not yet openly admitted your problem, which is why obsessive thoughts keep swimming around your mind, wreaking more havoc with time. Trust me when I say that clarity and peace of mind will flow into your life once you accept you have a problem.

When you embrace a particular weakness or an issue you are facing, you get out of the 'denial' phase. Instead of continually denying that you have a problem, you accept that something isn't right and requires your attention. This acceptance shifts your focus from feeling upset over the problem, to finding a solution, which turns you into a more solution-focused person who deals with the overthinking habit.

To accept the problem, here is what you need to do:

- Focus on inputting entries in a journal about your overthinking habit, what you've observed about it overtime, and what signs you can depict from it.

- Go through every account peacefully and reflect on how you often overthink.

- As you reflect on the instances when you have obsessive thoughts and over-scrutinised situations without taking any meaningful action, verbally accept that you overthink.

- You can also create an acceptance statement such as, "I accept that I overthink", "I am prone to overthinking", or something along those lines. Keep the suggestion short and free from any negative words such as, "I am sad that I overthink". This statement should only show your acceptance of the problem.

- Say it aloud a few times until you will feel the realisation sinking in. If you feel compelled to do so, you can also write it down.

Practice this little exercise daily for a couple of days so you can completely accept that you have an issue you need to address and tackle.

2: Set an intention to fix the problem

Once you have accepted the problem, start looking out for it. Can you remember a time when you wanted to improve a certain skill, or take up a new hobby, and you decided to take action to improve them?

Similarly, after accepting that you overthink, you have to create a positive intention to manage the issue. Here's how to go about it:

- Reflect on the problem and think about how you wish to overcome it.

- Create a concise and positive statement that reflects your intention to overcome the issue, and couple it to the previous statement about your acceptance of the problem. For example, "I overthink, and I am committed to resolving it," or "I overthink, and now I'm working to improve it." When you accept the problem and show an urge to resolve it, you motivate yourself to take charge of the situation and make things happen.

- As was the case with the earlier statement, repeat the suggestion out loud at least ten times. Say every word confidently with a smile on your face to send the subconscious mind a signal that you mean what you're saying.

- You can even write down the suggestion as you speak it to reinforce its effectiveness and better embed it in your subconscious mind.

Within a few minutes of practicing this, you will feel more enthusiastic about solving your issue and feel a sense of drive to work on it. Commit to practicing this exercise at least twice daily for a week or two to rewire yourself to think positively about your problem and start actively working on it.

When repeated frequently, positive statements become a part of your internal program. Whatever you focus on and believe to be true turns into your beliefs. When you repeat a positive suggestion, you affirm something positive to yourself, which allows you to change unhealthy beliefs into healthy, positive ones.

As your beliefs improve, so do your focus levels; you start paying more attention to the things that truly matter. Instead of getting consumed by worry, you become motivated to save yourself and work towards overcoming overthinking tendencies. Hence, stick to this practice to remind yourself of your commitment and become more invested in it each day.

3: Dig out your WHYs

"The key to being happy is knowing you have the power to choose what to accept and what to let go."

Dodinsky

In this journey we call life, we are all striving to be happy. At the bottom of all the endeavors we partake in and what pursuits we follow is the desire to be happier humans.

Similarly, you want to let go of your overthinking habit to find peace and happiness, which you need and deserve.

The best way to fulfill any goal is to have compelling reasons associated with it. You need to have the drive, motivation, and zeal to embark on a journey and make it to the finish line. Without that drive, you will struggle with sticking to it for the long haul.

It so often happens that when we start a pursuit, we find ourselves quitting it midway. Sometimes, we feel disconnected from it, find it too difficult to complete, don't know if it is the right voyage to embark on, feel we don't have what it takes to make it to the end, and at other times, we feel it is too early to pursue that endeavor. We often have many reasons or, undoubtedly, excuses to justify quitting our goals and pursuits halfway through.

In some cases, the reasons are justified, but in most cases, they are not. These issues boil down to the absence of our compelling WHYs that can help us stick to and complete our goals.

- *You feel disconnected from a goal because you never explored why it matters to you in the first place and whether it is the right goal for you.*

- *You find the journey too challenging to stick to because you don't truly figure out the value it adds to your life.*

- *You feel as though you lack the capabilities to accomplish a goal because you have never identified why it breathes fire into your life. Had you figured those out, you would feel increasingly motivated to develop the right skills for it.*

- *You feel the goal is not right for you, or it's too early to take up a pursuit because you did not pause to reflect on the meaning behind it.*

You are likely to feel the same way about your goal of overcoming overthinking. Every goal is difficult in its own way. Since this one directly relates to the way you think and feel, it will be a little challenging to talk yourself out of a habit you have nurtured for years.

By now, you know how hard it is to shut up your mind. It just does not abide by your rules and is not as obedient as you want it to be because it has learned to fire up thoughts in all directions over the years.

Does that mean you will never find solace from your racing state of mind? Of course, not! It only means that you need to work a little harder to accomplish your goal of silencing chaotic thoughts. Instead of just setting the intention to soothe your mind and break free of the vicious cycle of overanalysing everything, you have to support the intention with your compelling WHYs.

These 'WHYs' are the reasons you want to bring about this change, the reasons why you cannot stay stuck with a monkey mind long term, the reasons why you want to find peace, and the reasons why you must break this unhealthy habit for good.

Here is how you can dig out your compelling WHYs:

- Sit down somewhere quiet with a journal in hand; a peaceful location makes it easier to reflect on your thoughts.

- Think of your intention to quieten your racing mind and read it aloud a few times.

- Reflect on your life's current state and how it is not as you want it to be. Do you feel chaotic, highly-stressed, unable to make time for your loved ones, unproductive, unfocused, or unable to follow through with your important goals? Think about everything that seems wrong or out of place in your life.

- It is best to write down your feelings in detail or talk about them and record yourself expressing your concerns. It is important to let it all out so you can vent your frustrations. Plus, these accounts help you keep track of your feelings so that you can go through them whenever you lose the motivation to fulfill your commitment.

- Next, close your eyes and imagine a life of peace and tranquility. Think about a time where you could do whatever you want, a time where you focus on the task at hand without getting pulled into negative thinking by meaningless thoughts, and a time where you don't feel anxious, frustrated, or depressed. Create a mental picture of that in your mind, describe it in a written account, or record yourself speaking about your ideal life free from overthinking.

- From this account, find compelling reasons WHY you wish to quit this habit for good. What are the reasons driving your desire to work on this goal? Why do you need to stick to this commitment and actualise it? Why do you want to stop overthinking? What value will that add to your life? And how will doing so improve your overall quality of life?

- As usual, write all of that down in bullet points, going through the account as many times as needed, identifying your compelling reasons.

- Copying these reasons and putting them up in at least two prominent places in your house, such as your mirror and fridge, will provide you with gentle reminders of why you need to live in the present and worry less about the past or future.

With your reasons in place, ensure that you reflect on them daily to strengthen your commitment to your goal and stay true to it.

4: Create a SMART goal centered on overcoming overthinking

Besides not having compelling WHYs, a few other reasons why we lose sight of our goals is because they are not specific, measurable, attainable, realistic, and attached to a deadline.

Naturally, if your goal is vague, you feel confused about what you are trying to achieve. If you don't know how to measure your performance, you won't know whether you are on the right track. If a goal isn't attainable, you may struggle to find resources to use to set it. If it does not feel realistic enough, you are likely to avoid setting and pursuing it. And lastly, If it does not have a start and end date, you may procrastinate working on it.

By reading through these, you may resonate with why you haven't completed or achieved your past goals; the problems that make it difficult to accomplish your desires come with a simple and effective solution: *SMART*.

SMART is a handy goal-setting tool that allows you to set specific, measurable, attainable, realistic, and timely goals—each initial taking up an element. All your problems regarding not having a meaningful goal get solved by this handy trick.

Here is how you can set a SMART goal regarding your commitment to shutting up your mind that does not stop overthinking.

- **Make the Goal Specific:** A specific goal specifies what you want. "To be healthy" isn't as specific as a goal that states, "*I want to start eating healthy and exercise daily*". While being healthy only describes your intention to be so, the second example clearly states what you want. In terms of overthinking, a specific and clear goal could be, "*I want to overcome my habit of overthinking so I can be peaceful*" or "*I want to break my habit of overthinking about my relationships*". Every likelihood is that you don't overthink everything; you only overthink certain aspects of your life. In that case, identify the kind of things you overthink so you know what not to worry about. For instance, if you stress about how your kids' fair while in school, your goal could be, "*I am working on overcoming my habit* *of overthinking about my kids' welfare while they're in school"*. Try to make your goal as specific as possible to ensure that you target the exact area you want to improve.

- **Make the Goal Measurable:** How you intend to measure your performance and progress towards a goal makes it easier to stick to. To gauge whether you are achieving your target of losing 10 pounds in 3 months, you can use a scale to measure your weight and a tape measure to check your waist, hip, and other measurements. Similarly, there needs to be some measurement metric in place to gauge whether you are overthinking less than before. In this case, you could use your performance at a task, how peaceful you feel, a lowered sense of body pains and a measurement of your stress levels, to measure your performance at the goal. To track these changes, you could rate them on a 1-10 basis. For example, if your anxiety is usually at an 8, after being mindful of your overthinking, you may feel as if it has reduced to a 6. Noticing these changes allows you to see your development overtime, which increases your motivation to continue towards your goals.

- **Make the Goal Attainable:** An attainable goal is one set using resources that are at your disposal. Mostly, when we set a goal, we aspire to have an ideal situation to accomplish it. Starting your restaurant when you have £1 million is ideal. Losing weight with the help of an expert fitness trainer and a membership to the best gym would be amazing. That said, we don't always have access to these resources. Does that keep the motivated ones from fulfilling their dreams? The answer is 'no.' The truth is, you can achieve whatever you want if you start with what you have available right now.

In the case of shutting up your overthinking mind, you may think that you will start working on the goal once you get a good job or pay off your debts because these are the primary concerns worrying you at the moment. Perhaps you think you can only attain peace and harmony if you work alongside a spiritual healer or get guidance from a meditation practitioner or life coach.

While these are all great, you may not have the funds, time, energy, or space to pursue them. These limitations should not keep you from being serene. Based on your situation, set an attainable goal by thinking of how you can start working on actualising your commitment.

For instance, you can ask a friend to remind you to stay committed to your goal. You can set reminders on your phone to take breaks from overthinking. You can use guided meditations online to learn how to meditate and stay peaceful. Most importantly, you have this book by your side to encourage you to start this pursuit and fulfill it. Setting an attainable goal is one of the worst-kept secrets to massive success in whatever you're undertaking.

- **Time-bound/ Timely Goals:** A time-bound goal has a start and end date. Think of all the times you have decided to eat healthily but never had a starting date, or all the times you decided to start your own business but did not give yourself a deadline. It is quite likely you never got started with your pursuits, let alone finishing them. You don't want that happening this time around, right? In that case, the best way to accomplish something you set your mind to, is to set a timely goal; you can do this through timeline development. If you feel you need a day or two to prepare yourself to get started with the goal, set a date for two days from now. You could say, "From 10th February, I'll start working on improving my habit of overthinking and will reduce it to about 20% by the end of March". Make sure to attach a start date to all your aims to ensure that you know when you must begin working on it to avoid procrastinating. In parallel, have a deadline. Ensure you know when it is due, and work actively towards it.

Work on all these steps one by one, so you have a comprehensive and easy-to-follow SMART goal ready. Like before, write it all down. It is not possible to memorise everything, especially because we experience 50,000 to 70,000 thoughts every day. You may have an impeccable memory, but it is human to forget some things.

Action step

Start actioning and implementing these guidelines as soon as possible. Remember, the sooner, the better. Moreover, work on them every day to keep everything in perspective and be dedicated your commitment.

Since you have taken the first step towards your growth, let us move to the next one. After setting your intention and goal to turn down the volume of the mind, it is time to have a plan, a series of activities, and techniques you can use to achieve that goal.

From the next chapter onwards, we shall discuss many wonderful strategies, tips and ticks you can use to overpower disturbing thoughts and anxiety they can often cause. These approaches will begin to infuse peace, joy, and warmth into your life, helping you start feeling empowered and joyous.

Please read through all of them in detail, try them one by one, and see what works for you. Once you learn these strategies, create a personal toolkit you can practice daily to overcome stresses and constraints that keep you from being happy.

To achieve compound, lasting results, you need to start building habits. We are all creatures of habit. Everything we do consistently boils down to the habits we have created over the years. As a result, you overthink because you have trained yourself to behave that way. To let go of that behaviour, you need to set new, healthy habits that replace the negative ones.

Without further ado, let us move towards our first set of personal development habits that will help you switch off the chatter in your head, beginning with mindfulness.

Chapter 6: Master the Art of Mindfulness

Best-selling author and spiritual teacher Eckhart Tolle once said:

"Wherever you are, be there totally."

Every day, we have scores of things to do: cleaning, making food, running to work, doing the laundry or even if it doesn't seem like a task - catching up with friends: in essence, our plate is almost always full. However, if we analyse our level of involvement and presence in a task, we often realise it's not up to the mark.

For example, you may be researching topics for your presentation, but at the same time thinking about why a particular friend hasn't called you like they said they would. You may be sitting down with family members but at the same time worrying about how you will perform in your upcoming job interview.

Whatever we are doing, we are not always 100% present in it. We are often emotionally and mentally absent in our tasks; we are what psychologists and mystics call *forgetful of the present moment.*

This tendency to forget the present and rehash the past or fixate on the future tends to become stronger when we overthink. When your thoughts are running at a pace of 100 miles a second, naturally, you think more about the what-ifs, buts, and what could go wrong.

As upsetting and annoying as the situation can be, like everything else, it has a solution, one that is quite effective and lasting: mindfulness!

Mindfulness: The Surefire Antidote to Overthinking

Mindfulness refers to your ability to be completely at one with and connected to the present moment. It's being fully aware of who you are, where you are, what you're doing, and being in the here and now instead of feeling overwhelmed by what has or may happen.

Contrary to popular belief, mindfulness is a very simple and straightforward concept. It simply suggests that you pay complete attention to whatever happens around you, how you behave in the situation, your immediate environment, and every emotion you experience as a result. While this may seem trivial, the fact is that quite often, we veer from whatever we do during the present moment.

What Happens When We Are Not Mindful?

One minute, you may be analysing your business accounts, the next, your mind has taken a flight. A bit like when you're reading, it could be a sentance a paragraph or more, when you next try and recall what you've just read, you struggle as your mind was overloaded by other thoughts. You may have been reading, but you were mindlessly reading and not taking anything in. Which more often than not, means you have to read it again. You may have even done it in this book. When doing things mindlessly, you lose touch with your task, thoughts, body, and in a matter of seconds, you become engrossed in obsessive thoughts.

These thoughts often relate to something that has already happened or something that may happen, the odds of which may even not be too high. What happens as a result? Yes, you may become stressed and anxious. How pleasant would life become if you just lived in the moment and did not have to worry about these things? Mindfulness makes that possible.

When you become anxious, you tend to react to the situation. Instead of accepting whatever happens as it happens— mindfulness—, you snap to it. The instant you snap to something, your thoughts become clouded with intense emotions and irrational thoughts.

Instead of thinking straight and doing what you need to do, you employ erratic reasoning; you may even jump to making hasty, rash decisions that impact your general well-being. Fortunately, mindfulness can antidote that by equipping you with the capacity to make quick, rational decisions without obsessing over pointless thoughts.

Perhaps you are planning a birthday for a friend with other friends, and one of them mentions seeing your ex-partner with someone new. Ideally and reasonably, you would be capable of accepting the interaction as a casual instance. However, because of being mindless, you instantly read too much into it. You immediately become engulfed in memories and thoughts of your ex.

In such an instance, had you been mindful, you would have accepted your partner moving on as a normal occurrence. You would acknowledge your feelings of judgment, and maybe even jealousy, tune into your emotions and body, take a deep breath or two, and very tactfully steer the conversation back to planning the party, which is the issue at hand.

Let us look at another example that will help you understand how forgetfulness, aka mindlessness, keeps you from thinking and acting rationally.

Perhaps you have just started a home baking business and are looking to cater to big events. You get several offers from some big companies, but just as you are going through those messages, you see one from your parent, whom you stopped talking to years ago due to a family dispute.

That message calls up painful memories, making you ignore the messages you should be reading and responding to in the present. Consequently, you forget about your business agendas, let go of opportunities, and because of overthinking, you rehash the painful past.

Such situations resonate with many of us. On occasions, we forget what we're doing and get carried away by a wave of thoughts of the past or future, completely ignoring what we were doing in the present moment.

There have been many instances when we overreacted to our angry, fearful, surprising, envyous, and stressful emotions, instead of accepting them as they are and letting them settle down before deciding which step to take forward.

Let's contrast by discussing what happens when we are mindful

How Mindfulness Enhances Our Lives

Bhante Henepola Gunaratana, a Sri Lankan Theravada Buddhist monk and a mystic, once said:

"Mindfulness gives you time. Time gives you choices. Choices, skillfully made, lead to freedom."

This profound quote clearly and explicitly defines how our lives improve when we become mindful.

Mindfulness snaps you back from all the places far and wide that you drift off to when you let your awareness slip away from the present moment. When you're mindful, instead of wandering off into thought, you stay connected to the present moment.

Let us look at what happens when you pay full attention to what you are doing:

- When you focus on the right now, you do it with increased focus and attention. If you are cutting vegetables, you cut them consciously and attentively, doing the same task in only a few minutes instead of doing it in 20 minutes had you been using your phone simultaneously or fretting about a future concern.

- If you have a worthwhile thought in that time and choose to reflect on it, you do that very consciously too. Let's take an instance where you just got an idea, instead of thinking about it as you reply to emails, you should make a note of the idea and come back to it later when you have time to sit down and explore it deeply.

Making a note prevents your brain from rehearsing the thought repeatedly, making your present thoughts focused.

- When you solely think about one particular thought or task at a time, you can analyse it more consciously, peacefully, and attentively. You can explore every aspect, get a better perspective, re-center yourself, and make the right choice. You don't rush to make a decision, but you take your time with every experience and interaction and explore it fully to put your best foot forward.

- You also become better tuned into your emotions and understand them instead of reacting to them. For instance, let's assume you are angry because your partner invited their friends over for dinner without discussing it with you. Mindfulness helps you accept your anger as a reaction to the surprise, but instead of yelling at your partner or showing your resentment in front of the guests, you choose to let it pass instead of reacting to it. Being this accepting of your emotions and then allowing them to subside slowly gives you time to cool off and respond to the situation more productively and with a clear mind. In this case, after the guests leave, you may decide to engage your partner in a discussion on the importance of communication, and explain your emotions to them in a calm manner.

- Instead of disregarding everything that does not make sense to you or does not conform to the societal norms, you start accepting your thoughts, emotions, aspirations, and ambitions as a part of you. You may have felt strongly about a particular social construct, but you allow yourself to get consumed by consumerism and media biases which never allow you to follow what your heart truly wants. Mindfulness helps you understand that only your present matters, which allows you to stop letting your past or future rule your thoughts. You just let yourself become one with the moment, allowing clarity to flow in as a result.

- You stop labeling your emotions and feelings as good and bad, or right and wrong. Instead, you accept them as they are without reacting to them. When you get angry with those you live with about cleanliness, you accept the anger. When you feel envious of your friend getting their dream job while you haven't found your passion, you accept it for what it is. These are your emotions, they are valid, and you accept them as they are without blowing them out of proportion. You have control over what you think and what you project on others.

As you learn to embrace your emotions, you also learn to stop making a mountain out of a molehill of everything. You calm yourself down whenever an intense emotion stirs up, allow it to cool off, and then reflect on it to identify the best way to go forward. If you feel jealous of your friends relationship, you contemplate why you feel this way, understand that it boils down to how you approach your relationships. In this case, think of the SMART goals we explained earlier and then create a plan to achieve the goal.

Most importantly, you start to gain a deeper insight into who you are as a person, and what you want in life. Sadly, many of us live hectic, twisted lives from one beep of alarm to another, because of which we may may feel lonely, disconnected, and hurt. We don't know where we're going yet, but we're always on the run. Mindfulness offers you the freedom to stop running. It disconnects you from everything else, allowing you to connect with who you are. Once that magic happens, your life automatically becomes streamlined. You find yourself. You know your inner calling. You identify your life's vision, and you start taking steps towards a more fulfilling, meaningful life.

Wow! Just writing this account has charged me up. We miss out on so much in life, because we are forgetful of the moment. We don't seem to live our full potential because we don't live in the moment. We feel rattled because we are not mindful.

How about we change that for the better?

Together, let's train our minds to be more self-assuring and calm by being in the moment, ensuring all meaningless worries can quietly exit your system, allowing you to breathe in peace once and for all.

Let's discuss how to attain a harmonious and mindful state of mind.

1: Begin by taking short mindfulness breaks

You cannot become instantly mindful. It takes time, patience, practice, and consistency. That doesn't mean you can't get there; you can, and this journey starts with taking baby steps.

Begin by taking short mindfulness breaks throughout the day where you do nothing but allow yourself to be in the present moment. Doing this sounds difficult, especially since we have grown accustomed to multitasking.

When you're reading and texting, cooking and calling a friend, driving and listening to music, planning your week ahead and brainstorming a new idea, you aren't doing one thing at a time.

Here's what you can do to change this dynamic:

- Set reminders on your phone for every 3 hours to take just a 1-minute mindfulness break. Yep, that's it; in a day, you'll have about 4 to 6 mindfulness breaks of just one minute each. Not too long, right! But it will be powerful enough to help you calm down and ease stress.

- When your phone beeps, reminding you of the break, stop doing whatever you are doing. If you were writing a Facebook post, texting a friend, creating a creative for a client, or sorting out containers in the cupboard, stop doing it for the next minute.

- Sit comfortably on the couch, or stay wherever you are and set a timer for a minute.

- Take one deep breath, and let yourself go. Focus on your breathing; allow the air to enter your nose and slowly exit through your mouth.

- You may experience some thoughts instantly. When you do, very gently shake them off. Say something calming, such as, "I am here in this moment, embracing it fully".

Chant this mantra out loud, or if you can't, in your head a few times, and slowly allow yourself to focus on the moment.

- Focusing on the moment means you do nothing, think nothing, feel nothing, but that very moment. It may be challenging to experience that the first day, but you may start to feel new, positive sensations after a few days of consistent practice.

- When your timer beeps, do not rush to do whatever you were doing earlier; stay put for a few moments and revel in just being in the here and now.

- Once a few moments have passed, slowly get up and return to the task at hand.

Make sure to take these very brief mindfulness breaks several times a day. On the third or fourth day, or even the first one, you will find yourself slowing down and not feeling as rushed as you felt before.

With time, preferably after 2 to 3 weeks, slowly increase your mindfulness-based breaks to 2 - 3 minutes, giving yourself a chance to relax for a slightly longer period. The more you work on the practice, the faster you pave the way for the state of mindfulness, and the easier life becomes for you.

As you are taking these mindfulness breaks for no longer than a couple of minutes, it won't sacrifice the task at hand. Change your mindset and stop thinking that taking time away from something is negative and unproductive. If you have learned anything by now, it's to realise that you come first, and once you begin to believe it deeply, the quality of the task you were completing more often than not, improves along with your well-being.

2: *Add in Mindfulness-Based Breathing Meditation*

Life quickly becomes beautiful when you slow down and enjoy the serenity of it. Meditation makes this transition easier for you by allowing you to focus on just one thing at a time.

While many people refer to it as a tool to attain mindfulness, renowned mystic Sadhguru believes it is not a practice you can do, but a state you can be in. In one of his most famous quotes, he states, *"You cannot do meditation, but you can become meditative."*

According to Sadhguru, meditation is akin to a quality or virtue that you develop with time when you go beyond the dimensions of your body, mind, and spirit and unite yourself with the moment.

When you slowly cultivate a connection between your mind, energy, body, and emotions to a level of maturity, you stop fighting things that happen to you and around you. You let everything be and become meditative. Being meditative is similar to how plants and flowers start sprouting out of soil that is kept fertile, given sufficient water and sunlight.

When you are meditative, you stop fixating on the past or future and allow yourself to flow within the present moment. Everything that has happened or may happen stops bothering you because your concern only lies in the present, and even then, you stop fretting about perfecting everything.

This state of serenity and harmony with the moment infuses more wisdom, clarity, and stillness in your life, helping you slow down your racing mind.

While there are many ways to meditate, an easy-to-practice and straightforward exercise is '*mindfulness-based breathing meditation.*' Here's how you can practice it in your everyday life:

- Look for a neat, decluttered, and noise-free place to practice peaceful meditation. This could be your garden, bedroom, a nook in your house, or even somewhere outdoors away from your home. If you're new to meditation, it is best to find a spot that you can access daily to cultivate punctuality and regularity without any background noise or distraction.

- Once you have one, set down your yoga mat or sit on the floor with your legs crossed or extended out in front of you. If that doesn't work, sit on a chair or lie on your back.

- Set a timer for 2 minutes and close your eyes.

- Breathe in your natural manner; you do not need to lengthen and deepen your breath right now.

- Inhale through your nose, and watch your breath as it enters your body. Try to stay with it every second so you can map its journey from your nostrils to your abdomen.

- As you are ready to exhale, do so very consciously and observe your breath again, and just as it is about to exit your body, let it do so through your mouth.

- Observe your breath in this manner for about 5 to 10 breaths or until you start becoming more aware of it.

- When you've sunk deeper into present awareness, start noticing any bodily sensations that you can sense. The rising and falling of your belly, your nostrils as they inflate and deflate, any heating sensation in your legs, even any pain, anything that you can observe. Pay attention to it, and use it to tune in to your body more profoundly.

- Continue doing that for two full minutes.

- When the timer ends, gently open your eyes and let your awareness settle into the environment around you.

- You will feel more settled and calmer than before. This feeling will keep growing and deepening as you continue meditating this way.

After a few days, you can start deepening your breath. Inhale to a count of 5, hold your breath for 5, and release it to a count of 7. We inhale more when we feel frustrated and anxious; exhaling more air naturally calms us down.

As you inhale and exhale deeply, try to unite your attention and breath, thus observing it fully and using the breath to anchor yourself to the now. This practice effectively relaxes your stressed mind and creates some space between your thoughts, allowing you to think mindfully, and understand the difference between those related to the past or future, and those related to the present.

During this practice of observing your breath and bodily sensations calmly, you will wander off in thought. It is bound to happen. When it does happen, do not fight the feeling. Let it be. It is all normal and perfectly fine. However, the instant you realise you have drifted off in thought, acknowledge that and gently bring your attention back to your breath. You can count your breath in your head, one inhalation and exhalation as one, second as two, and so on until you reach ten, and start counting again to better focus on it.

Just stick to the practice for two minutes, then gradually increase the duration to about 5 minutes, and then 10 minutes. However, even if you do it for 2 to 5 minutes a day, it is good enough to help you control your overthinking tendencies.

3: Work on every task singlehandedly and peacefully

Once you stick to the practices discussed above, you will gradually observe a newfound stillness making its way inside your body, soul, and mind. You may find yourself overthinking at times, but you will also quickly become aware of it and guide yourself to tune into your breath and body to unite with the moment.

When that happens, encourage yourself to start working on your tasks singlehandedly so you can gently guide your thoughts to stay in a single direction instead of going haywire.

Most of the time, we feel confused and overwhelmed because we worry about a gazillion things concurrently.

Trust me, you don't need to do everything all at once, and it is okay if some things get delayed. Instead of feeling extremely rushed and bewildered all the time, go easy on yourself.

- Every time you have to do something, say what you are doing out loud. If you are dusting the table, say, "I am dusting" or "I'm going to dust the table consciously".

- Once you have proclaimed what you are doing, start doing it slowly. Say you are mopping the floor, when you move the mop slowly, watch as it clears away a dark spot or dirt. Once the spot is clean, move to the next one, and so on.

- Try to engage all your five senses in the experiences by feeling how that task feels, tastes, sounds, smells, and how it appears. For instance, in the case of mopping the floor, notice how the mop's bar feels in your hands, observe how it clears one dirty spot after another, whiff the smell of the surface cleaner, maybe imagine its taste, and pay attention to the slightest of sounds you can hear at that time. The more you involve your senses in the experience, the more engrossed you become in it, and the better your attention diverts from the past or future, to the present.

- If at any point you feel flustered or lose track of your thoughts, take deep breaths as we have discussed above, count your breath, and bring your attention back to your breathing, body, and then the task at hand. It is okay to get distracted; you will soon reach the point when you no longer have to worry about this as much.

Make a conscious, concerted, and consistent effort to work on every task mindfully, whether it's doing groceries, having a video conference with your coworkers, writing a business report, arranging utensils in the cupboard, playing basketball with your friend, or listening to music.

The more mindfully you engage in a task, the more focused on the present moment you will stay, and the less you will worry about everything else.

4: Be mindful of your emotions and treat them with respect

We often let ourselves get carried away into thought because we read too much into our emotions.

If you remember only one thing from this book, let it be that an emotion is just an emotion, something you feel as a reaction to experiencing something, perhaps a thought, experience, or something else.

When you get something you have desired, you feel happy. When things fail to go as planned, you feel sad. When you feel hurt or ridiculed, anger kicks in, and when you lose something, dismay takes charge.

Emotions are like seasons; they come and go, which is how nature intended it and how things should be. If that's nature's way, why then do we feel a certain emotion for way too long when on average, an emotion has a lifespan of 12-15 minutes? That's because we hold on to it.

When you keep thinking about your anger, sadness, envy, fear, frustration, and other emotions, they balloon up into something monstrous. You then react to them, and the emotions get a bad label.

Beyond these seemingly negative emotions, the habit of holding on to and reacting to emotions makes you make irrational decisions, especially when you feel happy and excited.

You may have decided to get back together with an ex partner because the strong connection and love you once felt cannot leave your mind. The first few times seeing them may bring up positive feelings and emotions such as happiness and adoration, but when you dive into the real world (everyday life) you realise the reason you separated in the first place. The excitement and joy turns into dismay, frustration and sadness, and you get pulled towards stress, and naturally, your overthinking starts to do the rounds in your head.

Although you know what is right for you, theres often a battle with accepting strong emotions of the past, present or future.

This issue is quite severe, and sadly, not many of us realise it until we start to scrutinise it deeply. Since you now understand the ramifications of getting hooked to your emotions, let's discuss an antidote to the problem.

The solution is to learn to acknowledge your emotions, accept them as they are, take a break when you experience an intense emotion, treat it calmly and respectfully, and then very rationally respond to it.

Here's what you need to do:

Every time you experience a strong emotion, be it anger, envy, surprise, joy, fear, or anything else, excuse yourself from the situation. For instance, let's say you are in a team meeting, and your boss speaks very firmly with you and even ridicules you in front of the team.

Naturally, you feel upset. Notice your sadness kicking in, and ask to take a quick break to the bathroom. If you cannot get away at that instant, no matter what the situation is, just stay put and breathe deeply. Once you are out of the situation, carry out the following steps.

- When knee-deep in a situation that makes you feel an intense, overwhelming emotion, keep taking deep, calming breaths and focus on the moment using the strategies we discussed earlier.

- When you are alone, or even in a public place, acknowledge that you feel a certain way. Try to pinpoint the exact emotion you feel and name it. If it is anger, explore if it is real anger, or could it be sadness disguised as fury?

- Once you have identified the emotion, give it some time to settle down, and take deep breaths to cool down the intense emotion.

- During this time, you may experience some reactive thoughts that compel you to spring to action and behave hastily as a result. For example, if your boss reproved you, you may want to snap back rudely. If your friend belittled you, you might want to ridicule them. If your child started crying loudly in the supermarket, you might want to yell at them back. Control these urges by breathing deeply and calming and say things to yourself, such as, "I am calm", "I am peaceful", "I inhale peace and exhale stress". You will calm down if you concentrate on the present moment.

- You may also get an urge to label the emotion as good or bad. Control this urge too, and merely accept it as an emotion. Not reacting to it, not labeling it, and not blowing it out of proportion, is what it takes to treat it with respect and calmness.

- Once the emotion has subsided, which can be anywhere from 12 minutes, a couple of hours, or sometimes a few days, regardless, reflect on what it's trying to convey to you.

- Analyse the emotion objectively and find a way to respond to it. For example, if your boss has been reprimanding you frequently and you feel hurt and dissatisfied with the job, think of what you genuinely want. Do you want to quit your job, or do you want to convey your feelings to your boss? Are you genuinely happy with the job, or are you doing it just because it pays your bills? Contemplate along these lines until you find a healthy way to respond to the situation.

In every situation that causes a powerful emotion, give yourself time to cool down and then think of the best way to respond. The answers will come to you if you're willing to look for them, and they will be very rewarding because they will help you put your best foot forward.

As you start to understand and work on your emotions using this mindful approach, you'll find it very easy to control intense feelings and rampant thoughts quickly. Anger that previously used to stay with you for days, will now leave your system a lot faster.

Naturally, when the emotions and thoughts that once used to wreak havoc in your mind subside, you'll stop overthinking as well.

5: Learn to listen and observe mindfully

To make mindfulness part of every aspect of your life, start listening and observing things mindfully too.

Seeing and listening are two acts we engage in daily. In most of the things we do, we rely on our senses of sight and hearing to act in an appropriate way.

While we listen to and see things all the time, we mostly do so based on our preconceived notions. Because you don't like someone you work with, you may rarely acknowledge what they say and disregard them. When you see a man and woman holding hands, you immediately start imagining the two in a close, intimate relationship because that's how society portrays every romantic relationship.

The problem with seeing and listening to things this way is that it clouds your judgment. It makes you read too much into things, and consequently, you start overanalysing everything.

To stop doing that and start taking situations as they are so you listen and observe things with clarity, start training yourself to do both the acts consciously and nonjudgmentally.

This strategy helps you see and listen to everything with an open mind, which allows you to assess things objectively and make informed decisions. Naturally, when you make logical, more beneficial decisions, you have fewer regrets to hold on to and fewer tensions to obsess over.

Here's how you can do that:

Mindful observation

To become an aware observer:

- Pick any natural object you would like to observe mindfully. It could be a plant, a tree, an insect, a cloud or anything else you would like to observe.

- Set a timer for a few minutes, or observe without any limitations.

- Start watching any one aspect of the chosen object very cautiously. For example, if you're observing a cloud in the sky, pick any one side of it and look at it gently and with keen interest.

- There is no need to make any judgments about what you see. When you feel an urge to judge, control it by taking deep breaths, then continue examining the natural object.

- Whatever your observations are, write them down in your journal.

- Once you have observed one side of it, pick another angle and inspect it in detail.

- After a few minutes of careful examination, describe your findings as clearly as possible using words and adjectives that describe them best.

- Practice this exercise three to five times every week. If you can do it every day, the better off you'll be—and feel.

In a couple of weeks, you will start perceiving things and situations for what they are without labeling them as good or bad and without using your preconceived notions as grounds to analyse them.

You will start perceiving things objectively and accepting them as they are, which will slowly reduce your tendency to overthink. If something looks odd, so be it; you won't feel a deeply-seated urge to spend hours overanalysing it.

This practice also trains you to analyse different aspects of a situation, making it possible to consider multiple factors before deciding something. Naturally, the more well-thought-out your decisions are, the better you feel about them, and the fewer regrets you have.

Mindful listening

- You can select a natural sound to listen to carefully and observe, such as a bird's song, wind, rain, the ocean or a storm (you can either listen in real time or find a sound on youtube).

- However, if that isn't feasible for you, choose to listen to any song or instrumental music from an artist you don't often listen to or someone new to ensure you don't have any previously formed judgments about them. Also, select the musical piece from a genre you haven't heard or something you don't listen to frequently.

- Play the musical piece and listen to it very attentively.

- Pay attention to every note, beat, lyric, and sound you hear as curiously as possible.

- If at any point your attention swerves or you start forming judgments about the music, shake it off by taking deep breaths and counting your breath to bring your awareness back.

- Once you are back on track, keep listening to the musical piece with as much mindfulness as you can muster.

- When done with the practice, describe your analysis using appropriate words that best describe how you feel about it. For example, if the song was high-pitched, label it so instead of calling it weird or annoying. If the lyrics were vague, describe them as vague and lacking structure instead of writing "the lyricist does not know how to write songs".

- Go through your analysis after the practice.

Like mindful observation, carry out this practice 3 to 5 times every week, or for a few minutes daily.

Soon, you will start listening to and observing things neutrally. Whether you are listening to a conversation, a speech, a presentation, news on the TV, or even your inner voice, you will do so very keenly, peacefully, and nonjudgmentally.

As you become a more impartial and keen listener and observer, you will find it easy to analyse different things based on what you see and hear. Yes, you will use your knowledge and experience to make a calculated analysis. However, you won't go overboard with it because you will realise the importance of being mindful and in the here and now. This practice teaches you that and raises your mindfulness level by manifolds.

Action step

Remember that mindfulness is a way of life that encourages you to take life a moment at a time, thus ensuring you don't overwhelm yourself with the unknown or what doesn't matter.

It gives you the mental capacity to pay attention to the moment and everything in it that sparks joy for you. When that change happens, the habit of overanalysing every detail gets replaced by the act of mindfulness.

As you build this habit, start working on improving your perspective of situations, particularly your past and future.

Chapter 7: Improve Your Situational Perspective

Rafael E. Pino, a revered General Authority Seventy of The Church of Jesus Christ of Latter-day Saints, once said:

"Perspective is the way we see things when we look at them from a certain distance; it allows us to appreciate their value."

Putting things into perspective is the right way to assess any given situation and make the most of it. Unfortunately, when our thoughts start to meander into hills and valleys, and that too at an unimaginably fast pace, it becomes difficult to get a clear perspective of things. That's when you find yourself overanalysing and blowing things out of proportion.

Now that you are better aware of the art of mindfulness and are ideally working on attaining and sustaining that state of mind, you are at a much better place to improve your perspective of situations.

How Our Distorted Perspective of Situations Magnifies Our Problems

For someone who overthinks, it is very natural to magnify any given problem and turn it into a catastrophe.

Even though you and your partner had a little rift, you start imagining possibilities of breaking up for good and becoming alone as a result.

If you did not get a certain dream job you interviewed for last week, you conclude that you may not find a job you fully enjoy and become demotivated by the fact.

Similarly, you may continue thinking about how disturbing memories of the past remain present and painful, even if you believe enough time has passed for them to have died down.

Yes, certain wounds never truly heal, and some agony associated with them persists no matter how much time has passed. However, the wound develops scabs when you keep poking and scratching at it.

When you accept something as the past, encourage yourself to stop consciously thinking about it, and train yourself to move on, the pain will eventually subside. The wound heals slowly and gets renewed by fresh skin. The scar remains, yes, but the aching diminishes. That is how we heal and how life goes on.

To ensure that you stop feeling sore about the past or become unbearably uneasy about the future, you need to accept things as they are and improve your perspective of the situation.

Let's discuss how you can do that:

1: Let it all out

Philosopher, spiritual teacher, religious leader, and meditator Buddha once said:

"You can only lose what you cling to"

While you may feel that clinging to your past way of thinking is important to ensure you don't forget the memories, you fail to realise that doing so only makes you lose the present moment.

Worrying about the past hasn't done you any good, nor has it done anything for you. If it had, or if it could, you would be happy now. Since you may feel you aren't as happy as you could be, you should realise and accept that clinging to your past won't improve your life in any tangible way. It will only keep you from moving forward.

To move on peacefully, start letting it all out to accept your past and make peace with it. That is one of the key steps to coming to terms with what has happened to live freely.

Here is what you can do:

- Curve out a 10-20 minute window of your time every day to journal your thoughts and feelings about your past. Right now, we are sticking to the past so let us discuss that only. A later part of this chapter shall tackle concerns of the future.

- Think of a past event that continues hurting you to this day, then describe it as well as possible. This step will be challenging as it forces you to rehash any deep memories you have suppressed over the years. However, to face the problem head-on and banish overthinking this memory, you will need to set it free.

- If you are not in the mood to write a very detailed account straight away, go for a short one, but ensure that you write it all out when you are ready. Even writing small amounts—at first—will allow you to come to terms with the memory, as it may not have left your mind since the event occurred.

- You can write it in a journal, on your phone, tablet, or any other device.

- Describe your feelings about why that particular event disturbs you to this day. What went wrong that day? Why do you keep thinking about it? What feelings did it trigger? Pour it all out.

- Just by writing it all down, you will feel relieved. We often stress too much about an event or certain feelings because we keep holding onto them inside ourselves. When you bring them out in the open, you'll feel relieved, and your urge to overthink will decrease too.

- Personal growth experts also propose deleting that account or burning that piece of paper once you have jotted down your feelings. This approach works for some people because burning or deleting the account signifies letting go, giving them a sense of peace, making them feel that they have deleted that part of their lives for good. However, this strategy may not work for everyone. Some of us want to keep track of our feelings to see how far we've come. If you're someone who would want to read an old journal entry to assess how you have progressed in life, it is okay to keep those accounts.

Once you have carried out this exercise, you will feel much better and more relaxed than before. Also, you will be in a better position emotionally and ready to forgive and forget your past. This simple logic is something you need to accept as soon as possible to walk yourself out of a tormenting life of overthinking and its ill effects.

2: *Make peace with your past*

Since you're now beginning to release all that pent-up tension, understand and accept that your past is just that: the past.

You cannot go back in time, at least not for now anyway; humanity is yet to invent a time travel device.

When something isn't humanly possible, why bother yourself so much about it? There's no reason to do that! Here's what you can do to make peace with your past, no matter how painful it was:

- Think of whatever painful memory from the past you wrote about earlier.

- Make a mental image of the pain and imagine it growing bigger.

- When the pain reaches its highest point, and you cannot take it anymore, imagine bursting the bubble open with a pin.

- As the bubble bursts, imagine the tiny fragments of your pain exiting your body.

- With that, keep saying, "I accept whatever happened and am ready to move on".

- If you wronged someone or someone else wronged you, forgive yourself and that person for the pain you went through. Forgiveness relieves toxic energy and brings light into your heart and life. Practice it often to stay peaceful.

Practice this exercise as often as needed to slowly soothe any remorse or agony from your mind and soul. Also, practice it while thinking of the routine mistakes and challenges you experience in your daily life to ensure that you take every moment that just happened as the past and use it as a trigger to focus on the present moment.

For example, if you punished your child unnecessarily, accept your mistake and take that occurrence as your past. Then apologise and commit to improving your emotional control and behaviour towards your child. The sooner you start implementing this strategic approach, the easier it shall be to live a peaceful life free from overthinking.

3: Assuage your future worries

Future concerns are one of the primary causes of overthinking, especially for those prone to anxiety. If you often feel anxious, it's probably because you often worry incessantly about your future.

As we have learned how to accept the past as something out of your control, you need to adopt the same attitude towards your future. By accepting the future as being out of your immediate control, you can alter your perspective towards different experiences and situations in life.

Here's what you can do to ease your anxiousness about future concerns caused by overthinking:

- Start by thinking about your most pressing future concerns and write them down in your journal.

- You can also talk to a trustworthy friend or family member about your worries. Make sure to ask them to refrain from judging you and just let you pour out your feelings.

- If you are writing them down, read them once you have finished.

- Have a very rational discussion with yourself on those feelings. Ask yourself if a concern is genuine. For instance, if you worry you won't have enough money to pay your bills, what are the odds of that happening? If the odds are slim, why are you fretting about it?

- Moreover, think of any available evidence that justifies your concern. If you think your current business will fail, which is what happened to your first one, think of what went wrong and instead, use it as a positive tool to apply those learnings to your current business. Also, think of other accomplishments, however small, and give yourself credit. As you think of these things, you'll feel better about yourself and realise that your future concerns lack authenticity.

- If your concerns relate to how someone behaves with you or how someone does not like you, reanalyse that situation but this time, using a mindfulness lens. When you objectively assess a situation, you end up realising that you were obsessing over something meaningless, and the person you are worried about may not even be thinking of you.

- If you are pouring your heart out to your friend, have this rational, objective discussion with them; it may help you resolve and understand your thought process clearer.

- As you complete this exercise, practice a soothing, positive affirmation to let go of unnecessary worries and invite peace into your heart. You can say, "I am peaceful and draw peace towards me", "I focus on the present only", "I live in the present, which makes my life beautiful", "I choose to be happy and peaceful in the here and now", or anything along these lines.

- Chant the affirmation aloud ten times with confidence and a relaxed smile on your face. In a matter of minutes, you should start feeling peaceful and relaxed.

Ensure you practice this routine regularly to help address some of your concerns and pave the way for a relaxed, peaceful life free from future concerns and anxious thoughts.

4: Practice positive self-talk

Self-talk refers to the way you talk to yourself. Whether out loud or in our heads, we all talk to ourselves, analyse situations, discuss ideas, and go through different memories with our inner selves.

This self-talk has a tone. It can be positive, negative, or even neutral. The neutral tone is often realistic and does not harm you; the positive tone uplifts your spirits, and the negative tone can eat away and lower your confidence.

Your self-talk is negative when you constantly remind yourself of any shortcomings and failures, doubt your capabilities, and keep thinking about the negatives attached to different situations.

This internal chatter with a somewhat undesirable tone does not do you any good. Even though you have built a habit of it and seem okay with it, deep down, it affects how you think, what you believe, and your actions in life.

Suggestions and thoughts like "Nothing can ever be right", "I'll probably fail at this", "I don't have what it takes to be successful", "My life is full of problems", and "I lack focus and commitment to do things right", are apt examples of negative self-talk.

The more you court such thoughts, the more they shape your beliefs, and the deeper you get pulled into overthinking, which leads to stress, anxiety, and even depression, keeping the vicious cycle alive. To break the cycle for good, train yourself to talk positively to yourself.

Change the tone of your internal chatter because the chatter will happen no matter what you do. Instead of allowing discouraging thoughts to demotivate you, create more uplifting ones.

If your perspective and attitude are negative, which boils down to your self-talk, you can improve and change the situation altogether by fixing the root cause.

Here is what you can do:

- Start becoming more conscious of your thoughts. The best way to do it is by being mindful of and noticing cues of hurt, agony, stress, anger, and frustration as they stir up inside you. If you feel hurt or disturbed, try to trace the situation or event that stirred up that feeling. When you engage in this process, you will identify something hurtful you said to yourself. You should write down this hurtful thing.

- For example, If you're considering pursuing an idea, deciding what to wear, or how to work on a certain project, scrutinise your thoughts. Do you notice any negative words in that self-talk? Did you say anything that convinces you that you cannot do something successfully? Did you highlight your weaknesses in a manner to belittle yourself? Write down whatever negative thoughts you discover.

- Acknowledge the thoughts, and be thankful to yourself for bringing the concerns into your conscious awareness.

- No matter what the negative thought is, reframe it into something more positive and realistic. For example, if you thought, "I won't be able to present well tomorrow", change it to, "Of course I can present the presentation amazingly. All I need to do is practice". Can you see how the second statement is full of hope and positivity? Instead of making you focus on your weakness, it guides you to focus on how you can improve the issue.

- Make a conscious effort to reframe your thoughts in this manner every time, but especially when you catch yourself engaging in negative self-talk. Each time you think negatively, you will be ready to counteract the toxic thought with something powerful and positive.

If you forget to carry out this practice throughout the day, take stock of some of your prominent thoughts and inner suggestions that you've noticed yourself say throughout your day or in life generally, and journal them in the evening.

One by one, swap all of them out with positive replacements, and chant those suggestions to rewire yourself to think positively. This approach helps you live more in the here and now, fretting less about the future.

5: *Reframe the problem*

Reframing is a beneficial technique that helps soothe your stressed nerves and talk yourself out of feeling miserable without downplaying your struggles.

We often continually worry about something trivial. Since we are in that 'worrying' state of mind, the issue seems to engrave itself to us at that time.

With that said, when some time passes and the sore wound heals a little, the pain diminishes and becomes stale. It stops bothering you as much as it used to because it is not fresh anymore. You have moved past the incident.

Sometimes, the problem is quite grave, and so are your concerns about it. That's not always the case. At times, we vex about inconsequential things for no solid reason. Because we have the habit of overthinking, want some attention, or because it seems significant to us at the time, we hold onto it tightly in a vice grip and let it consume our sanity.

Perhaps the fuss you made about your partner not consulting you before buying a new TV seems significant now but won't seem consequential later. Maybe all the arguments you had with your parents about persuing a certain career will seem insignificant later.

To mitigate your worries, start reframing your problems now so you can see them under a new light, preferably a humorous one, and stop fussing about things that should not truly matter.

Here's what you need to do to implement this strategy:

- Think of the problem you are obsessing over. You could be thinking of a job interview you have to take with an authority figure, about your current intimate relationship, or about how you were ghosted by a date.

- Create a mental picture of it as vividly as possible.

- Take a snapshot of that mental picture.

- Zoom in or out of it, add color to it, or keep it black and white.

- You can even add filters to it just like those available on Instagram or Snapchat.

- Put stickers, text, and other effects on it to make it as entertaining as possible. You are likely to feel more at ease from just doing this.

- Add a frame to it, and change its color to your liking. It can be black, blue, gold, copper, or any other color you want.

- Lastly, imagine putting it up in an art gallery where everyone comes in and admires this interesting or rather hilarious piece of art.

- View it from the perspective of a third person. When you do, it won't intimidate you as much as it did before.

- Also, ask yourself if the worry consuming you now will matter to you a few days or weeks from now. Look for the honest answer that comes from within. It is likely to be a 'no' in most cases. Accept that answer and commit to moving on peacefully.

Sometimes, all you need to do to relax is to take off the unnecessary light and attention from a situation. Reframing it helps you do the trick nicely, allowing you to loosen your grip and decongest your mind from circling thoughts to find solace in the present moment.

6: *Shift your focus*

Whatever you focus on becomes your reality. This universally accepted law applies to every aspect of your life too.

Feeling upset, miserable, and withdrawn from everything and everyone, is not because the universe hates you. Sadly, things are usually this way because you mainly focusing on the negatives in life.

Focusing on your problems like, missing out on a vacation, an unexpected challenge, not having a loving partner, the mistakes you made in the past, things that are missing or going wrong, and every other thing like that, only reminds you of your troubles.

Understandably, it can be tough to keep yourself sane when challenges seem to ambush you from every direction. However, fixating on the problems only brings more troubles your way.

The Law Of Attraction (LOA) has quite a role to play in this equation. Everything in this world, including all material and immaterial things, and yes, even your thoughts, are composed of energy.

As you already know, energy vibrates, and thus, naturally, everything made of energy vibrates at a certain frequency. That vibration moves out into the universe, attracting other things vibrating at more or less the same or a similar frequency.

This principle applies to our thoughts as well. When your thoughts vibrate, they move out into the universe, interacting with other thoughts, especially those vibrating at more or less the same frequency.

They then draw similar energies towards them, along with experiences, people, and situations tied to them. That explains why you attract more good experiences when you are happy, excited, energetic, and passionate, and why you only bring more problems your way when you are frustrated, annoyed, sad, and angry.

Emotions such as anger, fear, sadness, envy, and those alike come with a negative connotation, and low mood—negative thoughts have low energy vibrations. Nurturing them lowers your overall vibration, causing you to attract more situations of the same kind.

In contrast, positive thoughts and high-energy emotions such as happiness, excitement, passion, serenity, and hope have high energy vibrations. Thus, nurturing them raises your vibrational frequency too.

To bring desirable experiences your way, you need to nurture these emotions. One effective way of doing that is to shift your focus towards the good things in life.

Here's how you can do that with ease:

- Instead of fixating on the problem when you're stuck in a rut, think of the solution.

- First, calm yourself down by taking some deep breaths, then practice a positive affirmation to center your focus on your breath, body, and the present moment.

- When you feel better, mindful, and connected to the here and now, think of what the situation teaches you. For example, if you failed an exam, think of how you have another chance to improve your weak areas. If you did not get a promotion or pay rise, maybe look into other opportunities you can explore.

- Write down the lessons you distill, and also focus on the positives of the situation.

- As you do that, you automatically feel better about the problem and start worrying less about it.

Do you see how quickly and easily you shifted your focus and improved your mood? Well, that's the power of keeping your face towards the sun, keeping the shadows from intimidating you.

Action step

Remember that to nurture and grow a seedling into a plant, you need to water it daily, make sure it gets sufficient sunlight, and that the soil it is growing in is fertile enough to nourish it. Likewise, to continue improving your perspective towards life's problems, you need to work on all the approaches taught above consistently, to build a positive frame of mind, sustain it, and keep it growing.

The overarching goal is to improve your internal chatter [its tone] because the thoughts you feed yourself shape your reality. Thus, it's in your best interest to start feeding your mind happy, constructive ideas that motivate you to take similar actions.

Chapter 8: Start Taking Care of Yourself

American activist, author, and educator Parker Palmer once said:

"Self-care is never a selfish act—it is simply good stewardship of the only gift I have, the gift I was put on earth to offer to others."

Regrettably, many of us forget to take time for ourselves, and as the quote mentions, we see doing so as selfish.

We tend to make special exceptions and prioritise everything and everyone else but ourselves. This unhealthy attitude and practice can add to your problems.

We seem to easily make time for our work, family, friends, problems, career, and anything external from ourselves, but none for our needs – specifically our mental ones.

- *You may not know what you truly like.*

- *Perhaps you haven't engaged in an activity you enjoy for years.*

- *Maybe you haven't laughed out loud properly in months.*

- *You may not know what it feels like to be well-rested.*

- *And you may have never really sat down with yourself to deeply understand your emotions or reflect on your experiences so far, as you always seem to be rushing and thinking about 'what's next?'*

These issues only strengthen toxic thoughts, encouraging them to make more noise inside your mind. Consequently, overanalysing your problems leads to more overthinking, increasing feelings of stress as a result.

These issues, and an uncontrollable tendency to overthink, can easily stop bothering you once you start taking time to care for yourself.

How Self-Care Relieves Undue Worries

When we tend to everything around us, we somehow give up control over ourselves.

- *You may run around solely doing things for your children, as you see them as a priority.*

- *You may routinely do things for your partner to make them feel loved.*

- *You may continuously tend to your all boss' demands.*

- *You may pursue different career aspirations just to earn more money and live a better life.*

- *You may only watch movies your friends like.*

Naturally, with all such things happening in your life, you're bound to feel as if your choices and feelings don't matter, as those around you may fail to ask you what you want and feel like doing, which may result in feeling as though you don't get to decide how to live.

All such apprehensions, disturbances, and frustrations strengthen with time, turning into a vicious overthinking cycle. The more you think about them, the stronger and bigger they grow and develop into overthinking habits.

You know you deserve to have an opinion and have it listened to, but somehow you cannot work towards it. The truth is, only you can make it happen because this is your life, and your happiness is a choice you have to make. If you want a happy life, you have to create a happy life. That's how it works.

In previous chapters, we have discussed many ways to build an optimistic and mindful state that can help you remain calm and feel happy despite problems that come your way.

This chapter shall show you how caring for yourself can further strengthen an optimistic attitude towards life.

As humans we often seek external validation from others, and when we don't receive it as expected, we feel upset. However, when you care for yourself, you feel love from within. You feel happy and prioritised because you feel that you matter.

Wanting people to understand how much we need their support and care, we need to understand that unless you love, care, and respect yourself first, you will struggle to find others that do.

Quite often, the root cause of our overthinking is setting expectations for other people. We expect our loved ones to be as compassionate towards us as we are towards them. When that does not happen, we can feel hurt, making us obsess over these things.

Since overthinking stems from exhaustion and fatigue, you may notice that you overanalyse things more when feeling mentally and physically drained. You try to perfect the things around you and the outside world in the hopes of feeling better. What we don't realise is that true happiness and peace sparks from within you. You need to fix the internal elements before you can truly thrive.

Moreover, caring for yourself helps you frame your internal chatter positively. When you shower affection on yourself, you feel good, which improves your self-talk, making it possible to experience happiness in the present.

Now that you know this, you must commit to caring for yourself and prioritising you above everyone else. Doing so is in no way selfish. It is you looking out for yourself. Your sanity and joy depend on that, and it is high time you give yourself what you deserve.

Let's discuss some strategic approaches you can use to start caring for yourself better and gradually tune down all the thoughts that don't shut up and congest your mind.

1: Start focusing and dedicating enough time to sleep

The morning after staying awake for most of the night is never easy. You may lack concentration, feel sluggish, struggle with finding the right words to express yourself, and have increased irritability on the slightest hint of trouble.

When just one night of poor sleep negatively affects your day, imagine what effect lack of regular sleep has on your mood and thoughts.

There is clear evidence supporting the fact that a lack of sleep affects your health, lowers your energy levels, and puts you at risk of health issues such as heart disease. More studies conducted on the subject have shown that insufficient sleep can also lead to mental illness.

Michael C. Marino, the medical director of Geisinger Sleep Labs and D.O., found that thinking negatively once in a while is normal, especially if some serious problems are playing out in your life. However, if you constantly feel anxious and chronically overthink, a lack of sufficient sleep may be a key contributor.

Looking over the CDC reports, it's clear that one in every three adults do not get the recommended amount of sleep: 7 to 9 hours a night. As the findings revealed, chronic sleep deprivation could lead to increased negative thinking, chronic stress, anxiety, and depression, so why do we allow this to occur so frequently?

Dr. Marino strongly states that sleeping well helps combat negative, repetition, and chronic thinking. When you linger on unhelpful repetitive thoughts, negative thinking establishes a colony in your conscious mind.

Thinking that you don't contribute much to your loved ones or that you aren't doing well in life are examples of such thoughts. They don't serve any substantial purpose other than sabotaging your well-being and consequently laying the foundations for mental health disorders.

Researchers have discovered that those who often report sleep disturbances tend to have more negative thoughts and emotions. Many of us fixate on negative things more, a tendency that only aggravates when we don't sleep enough.

Think of one time you weren't well-rested and hadn't slept well in days. The days that followed that period were difficult, right? You may have obsessed over the little things. Your work productivity may have decreased, and when you spent time thinking, your thoughts might have been predominantly negative or side tracked.

The point of painting this picture is to show you that we tend to experience a wave of thoughts when we feel exhausted. A tired body leads to a tired mind and vice versa; a combination of the two only worsens your tendency to overthink.

As sad as this sounds, it comes with a very relaxing fix: more rest and sleep.

- Accept the mission of sleeping for no less than 7 hours a night, each night. Start by reminding yourself how much you need to sleep well, and when you're having trouble doing so, chant affirmations such as, "I sleep for 7 hours nightly". This suggestion rewires your brain to focus on the idea, leaving you feeling motivated to sleep well.

- Set a sleeping and rising time that gives you around 7 to 8 hours of sleep. Stick to this for about 3 to 4 weeks. Even if you cannot drift off to sleep right away, remember that our body clock takes a while to adjust to the new schedule, but rest reassured that you will achieve the goal successfully if you are consistent.

- Get into bed about 30 to 60 minutes before your sleep time and relax by reading a book, writing in your journal, listening to some soothing music, taking deep breaths, or reflecting on the day by giving gratitude to your body and mind.

- If you feel like it would help, about an hour before bedtime, shower with warm water or draw yourself a warm bath. It will help you unwind and prepare your body to relax and rest.

- When you lie down, turn your attention to the 3 B's, breath, body, and bed, this will allow you to focus on yourself and the present moment and keep your thoughts from wandering off to undesirable places.

- Avoid looking at any screens an hour before your bedtime. The blue rays emitted from these screens, especially laptops, smartphones, and tablets, disrupt your circadian rhythm—your body's natural sleep-regulating clock—messing up your sleep cycle.

Naturally, when you have a messed-up body clock, you struggle to initiate and maintain sleep. If it helps, put your phone and laptop away in a cabinet and lock it. Every time you feel compelled to use them, remind yourself of the importance of resting and allowing your body to refresh, then go back to bed. It will take you some attempts, but soon, you will become disciplined enough to pick up your phone only when it's necessary.

- Ensure your bed is comfortable, cozy-enough, and relaxing when you lie down. At times, an uncomfortable bed and mattress may be contributing to your poor sleep, so check and fix the issues if there are any.

- Also, ensure your room has a soothing sleep environment. The walls should block any unwanted outside noise, the room temperature must be just right, and the lighting mustn't be too harsh.

Your body and mind want to rest when the day ends. It is on you to provide it with that essential care, so start resting more to curb your overthinking to feel energised every day.

2: Become more physically active

Many of us don't realise this, but staying physically fit helps relieve stress and anxiety. Overwhelming and persistent toxic thoughts can lead to mental health problems. You may obsess over things you need not obsess over because you feel you have nothing else to do.

We mentioned earlier how worrying too much triggers the stress response in our bodies. The mind interprets your constant worry as a signal of threat and disturbance, which then directs your body to release more stress hormones. Since you are not experiencing any genuine threat but are only feeling this way, the overproduction of hormones released into your body results in a chemical imbalance. These chemical imbalances further exacerbate any anxiety and chronic overthinking you may be experiencing.

Sometimes we become lethargic and don't feel like doing anything at all. If we encourage ourselves to move around and become physically active, we can help counteract the chemical imbalance and depressive state of mind.

Exercise motivates the release of endorphins into your body. Endorphins are feel-good neurotransmitters that mingle with receptors in your brain to produce a euphoric high.

That high makes you feel good, provides an escape from your tensions, and makes you feel content that things are okay—or are going to be okay. Naturally, when you genuinely believe that, you feel stimulated to think and act positively, which consequently brings about a beautiful, positive difference in your life.

When we see people around us staying active daily, we immediately assume that they have little to no worries in their life, which usually isn't the case.

Upon talking to them, we find out that they are fighting many battles, including failed relationships, career problems, financial instability, and the likes. However, they still seem to move on with life because they believe in themselves.

Looking into their routines, you will discover that they habitually engage in physical activities like brisk walking, jogging, yoga, aerobics, cycling, swimming, or playing an active sport.

Physical activity does wonders to your body and mind. It energises you, builds your stamina, improves your mood, boosts your concentration and focus levels helping you think clearer, it also provides you with an opportunity to socialise with others.

Moreover, sometimes you overthink when you are brimming with energy that you need to burn off. Exercise gives you a healthy way to do that, which is why becoming active allows you to vent off that additional energy and relax your mind.

Now that you are more aware of the wonders of becoming physically active, here is what you can do to make exercise an integral part of your daily routine and part of your anti-overthinking campaign:

- Find any physical activity you feel excited about; it could be walking, running, cycling, pilates, kickboxing, anything you enjoy doing.

- Start doing that activity at any time of the day you're free. Make sure to select a time that you can stay consistent with regularly. If you go for a walk at 6pm for a couple of days, stick to it to build punctuality and consistency, more so in your mind. In a couple of weeks, your brain will start to associate walking with that time, and 6pm will start acting as a trigger to compel you to engage in the habit of walking.

- Start small. There is no need to exercise, walk, or run for straight 30 to 40 minutes on day one, especially if you have been stationary for a long time or are getting back to physical activity after having a break. Begin with doing it for 10 minutes only, and stick to the same duration for at least a week. Soon, your energy and motivation levels will increase, stimulating you to engage in the activity regularly.

- Once you start doing a physical activity for a few minutes a day, encourage yourself to do it for another 10 to 15 minutes at another time in the day. For example, if you're walking in the morning for 15 minutes, you could go cycling for 15 to 20 minutes in the evening. You can engage in the same activity every time, pick a different one for each day of the week, or alternate between two or more activities. Maybe Mondays are where you walk, Tuesdays you cycle, Wednesdays can be for yoga, and so on, or you can walk and jog the entire week. The idea is to become physically active; pick and choose whatever works for you.

- Playing a sport with some friends can bring more fun and excitement to your life. Play football with friends, have a tennis match with your partner, or join a badminton club, all of which also encourages you to socialise and make new friends at the same time.

- No matter which physical activity you engage in, slowly increase its duration. For instance, if you begin jogging for 10 minutes, increase it to 12 to 15 minutes after two weeks, and keep increasing the duration until you start exercising for a good 30 to 40 minutes a day.

- Once you get in the habit of staying more active, you can limit your physical activity to 3 to 4 times a week. However, if lightly exercising daily works well for you, go for it, but always listen to your body.

- As you exercise more, start to look for other ways to stay active throughout the day. For example, start using the stairs more often if you don't usually. Instead of cutting vegetables while sitting on the couch, stand to do the task. Instead of getting your groceries delivered, go and fetch them yourself; see walking down the aisle as an exercising opportunity. Every day has countless opportunities for us to become more active. If you start becoming more active consciously, you will begin to notice a remarkable difference in your mood and energy levels.

Yes, taking the first step to becoming more physically energised and stimulated is not easy, but trust me when I say that there is no going back for you once you take that step. An active lifestyle reaps so many rewards so, start exercising to create a healthier, more positive you!

3: Know your needs and prioritise them

Regrettably, many of us aren't aware of our needs. We say we are happy, but deep down, we feel dissatisfied. We talk about how important it is to live for ourselves, but somehow, there is an inner conflict with that as we don't live our lives on our terms.

Why does this happen? It happens because you never really stop to think about what you want and how you can actively pursue it.

Over time, we forget about our aspirations, hobbies, and passions and then wonder why our lives lack meaning and joy. When you disregard your urge to paint more, dance, read or travel, you ignore the fact that inside you exists a being who needs to feel alive, and their needs are more than just eating, sleeping, and going to work.

Since you may feel as though you haven't been treating yourself well for some time, unpleasant and unwanted thoughts may begin to creep into your mind, making it a landfill of thoughts that make your life more difficult.

It's okay; this happens to the best of us. What's not okay is to feel like that continuously and not commit to doing something about it.

You can improve that for the better by:

- Starting to make a list of all the activities and pursuits you wish to engage in from this moment onwards. Think deeply about what you want to do more, why that activity matters to you, then put it down on the list. Arrange these activities in descending order starting from the one you feel most passionate about, down to what excites you the least.

- In your daily routine, find some time, say 20 minutes, to engage in that activity. For example, if you enjoy reading, make time for that. If 20 minutes seem too challenging to manage, start with 10.

- Stick to one or two activities for a week, and then add another one in the third week. Taking this approach allows you to do something for yourself everyday that sparks inner joy and frees your mind from overthinking and negativity.

- Moreover, think of passions you wish to pursue and start engaging in them often to find your bliss.

As you engage in activities that bring you inner happiness, you start to forget about your unnecessary worries. Your new hobbies positively distract you from meaningless concerns, and soon happiness, peace, and serenity flow into your life.

4: Let others know you matter

We don't appreciate it when people disregard our feelings. We don't like feeling bombarded with a constant stream of new favors and requests from friends, family, and work colleagues. We don't want people to treat us as pushovers or take advantage of our kindness.

Although we don't want any of that, we don't realise that we're not sending other people the right messages.

- *We often say yes to everything others want, even when it doesn't bring us happiness.*

- *We go out of our way to help someone who often may disregard our feelings.*

- *We fail to communicate our concerns and needs openly.*

- *We rarely voice our thoughts and fears when needed.*

Don't we do all of that? Yes, we do, which is why we indirectly and unknowingly send the wrong messages to people, making them sometimes mistreat us.

We may lack setting boundaries in relationships. We may not prioritise ourselves. We may struggle to say 'no' when we need to, and we don't talk about how we feel.

Unfortunately, even after failing to do all this, we expect others to understand us. If we don't communicate with others the kind of treatment we're willing and unwilling to entertain, we end up in a cycle of doing things we don't want to do.

You can change that narrative and situation for the better by letting people know you truly matter:

- When engaging in a meaningful activity, make sure that everybody knows not to bother you, especially if that's your 'me-time.' For example, if your spouse asks you to make coffee while you're listening to your favorite music, let them know that you are busy, and can tend to their needs later. Every time you spend some quality me-time with yourself, don't allow anyone to bother you. Don't take calls or respond to messages, and stay off social media, thus devoting that time solely to yourself.

- Start saying 'no' to people who misuse and mistreat you. If a friend has a habit of frequently asking you for favors, like asking you to borrow money to pay their bills or even pick up their children from school, understand that they're leveraging your niceness, and it is time to stand up for yourself. Start saying 'no' to these people. Every unnecessary 'yes' you have said to your friend, a colleague, your boss, partner, neighbour, or anyone else, has paved the way for them to build up a habit of approaching you for favors. Many people who misuse you have developed this habit because your behaviour somehow encouraged them. Since you may enjoy the attention and affection—usually superficial— they shower on you when you please them, you perpetuate the habit, turning into a people pleaser. Though this idea may not sit well with you now, since you've become so deeply immersed in it, you struggle to jump out of the cycle. All of this contributes to your tendency to overthink. Ending it starts with being firm with those who use you. Start pulling back from it, and soon, they will start respecting you too.

- Speak up for your needs whenever needed. For example, if your partner is planning a vacation for the two of you, but you aren't too excited by the idea of going someplace warm like you do every time, let your partner know that this time you wish to go to a colder place. The fear of having a conflict with someone often keeps us from communicating our needs and concerns. While we seem okay with not voicing our opinions, we feel disheartened from within. It's wrong to expect your partner, friend, or any person to understand your feelings without you communicating with them. Not everyone has a strong sense of intuition. If you want other people to understand what you want, you have to say it loud and clear. Let others know that you want to express some concerns and wishes to them, and mindfully let it out. When you do, people will begin to understand your needs better and start to respect them.

- Start setting boundaries in every relationship you have. Boundary setting refers to setting limits, rules, and principles regarding what's acceptable and unacceptable to you in a relationship. Perhaps you don't appreciate it when your partner checks your phone without asking you, or when your colleague uses your things without your permission. If you don't communicate that concern to the other person, they won't know about it and shall continue doing so. Spend some time reflecting on what works for you and what doesn't when it comes to your key relationships. Also, reflect on the dynamics of every relationship and how you want things to be. Once you have that clarity, have a thorough discussion about it with the other person. After communicating your needs, ask them how they want things to be. Find some middle ground, and start working towards having the relationship you have defined. If you cannot find a middle ground in a particular relationship, and the other person does not understand your viewpoint, it is best to put your foot down there and then. It's not in your best interest to carry on with the relationship, only to end it many months or years later when you feel emotionally suffocated.

- Stop allowing people to manipulate you through emotional blackmailing. If someone asks you for a favor, but you refuse to carry it out, stand your ground. The other person may remind you of the times they've helped you, the terrible state they're in, or how their survival depends on your help. If this person has a habit of doing that every time they approach you with a request that you reject, understand that for what it is: emotional manipulation. Be firm with them, excuse yourself from the situation, and gradually distance yourself. Your gestures and behaviour will pass your message and save you from the person's blackmailing tendencies.

- For people whose toxicity weighs you down with their negative talk, reduce your interaction with them, and distance yourself from them altogether, whether that's your neighbour, colleague, sibling, friend, or even your parent. There's nothing wrong with doing what's right for your sanity to prevail. You are well aware of the dynamics of your different relationships and what weighs you down about them. Thus, only you can decide which relationship does or does not make you feel drained and hurt. Take your time when making this decision, and then make the final call. Trust me; it is okay not to want to be around many people who only sabotage your well-being and be around only a few who build you up.

It will take time to work on all these areas and make them constants in your life, but once that happens, your life will become more relaxed and pleasant. You will feel in control of your actions and decisions. You will feel loved and cared for by people who appreciate you. You will know you matter because you start to respect your needs.

All this boosts your self-esteem, helping you value yourself more and feel more confident in your ideas, actions, and endeavors. Consequently, that helps you progress in life and reduces your repetitive thoughts to a significant degree.

5: Build more relationships

You may have happy relationships in life but crave more. Perhaps you have a good circle of friends, but they are all your work buddies, so now you crave friends outside of work to have a better work-life balance.

Similarly, you may desire a partner who understands, accepts and loves you for who you are. However, since you may feel like you need to constantly change and your current relationship to be happy, it may lead you to experience emptiness in your heart and mind.

It is okay to want more relationships and crave the right sort of partnership or friendship. To experience that, you should start working towards that goal.

Here's how you can do that:

- Understand the need for the relationship you crave, and write down what you expect from it. For example, if you are looking for an adventurous person who shares your interest in exploring new places, write that down.

- Next, start looking for different avenues where you can find such people. You could attend meet-ups, conferences, social circles, parties, to meet like-minded people.

- You can even connect with many people online via groups on Facebook and communities on other social media platforms, that share your interests.

- Remember to be active while engaging with others to ensure that you find the right match.

6: Take care of your diet

While there are no superfoods associated with reasoning and reducing the intensity of chronic and obsessive thoughts, there are foods that can improve your overall emotional well-being. Adding these foods to your diet naturally boosts your happiness and enthusiasm levels. When you feel happy, you find it easier to fight repetitive, negative thoughts, allowing yourself to live more in the present moment.

Besides adding mood-improving foods to your diet, you also need to fix your eating habits. Skipping meals, eating in a rush, and over or undereating are unhealthy behaviours that affect your emotional and general well-being and could cause overthinking.

Here are some dietary changes you can make and things you could start doing now to keep yourself from overthinking:

- Reduce your intake of caffeinated beverages, and stick to about 100ml of them once or twice a day. Too much caffeine messes with stress levels in the body.

- Add foods loaded with antioxidants and B-vitamins to your diet. These include berries, bell peppers, avocado, and citrus fruits. Such foods can actively help improve your mood.

- Also, look to consume more lean cuts of meat, fresh fruits, and veggies. Notably, eating leafy greens, nuts, seeds, whole wheat goods, and organic dairy products will provide you with the recommended intake of proteins, carbs, good fats, minerals, vitamins, and fiber, allowing you to stay fit and healthy. When you get good nutrition, you automatically feel healthy and overcome irrationality, which is the essence of overthinking.

- Dairy-free, meat-free, and gluten-free options have proven to make a big difference in how your body feels and your mood. Even though you would benefit from making some changes, if you find it difficult do so gradually. For example, one day a week, you could eat meat-free. This way, you will slowly introduce healthier food options into your diet while still enjoying the things you love.

- Stop skipping meals, especially breakfast. Breakfast energises and prepares you for the day ahead. Pack your breakfast with nutritious foods rich in carbs and protein to ensure you get an energy-rich start to the day.

- Keep some healthy snacks with you at all times, especially when traveling. Feeling intensely hungry or having big gaps between your food intakes affects your sugar levels, which can make you cranky. When you are irritable, fixating on negative thoughts is near automatic.

- Drink 2 to 3 liters of clean, drinking water daily. 90% of all the chemical processes and reactions in your body need water. Staying hydrated keeps you energetic and active. Oppositely, dehydration can often be the cause of a lack of sensible reasoning.

Start working on your diet and nutrition today, as these simple tips can go a long way in reviving your sense of happiness and daily mood.

7: Reduce your workload

Being driven and ambitious about your work is healthy. What what's not healthy is letting your work get in the way of your sanity or living your life.

If your workload has a firm grip on your mind, keeps you occupied even after your office hours have ended, and does not let you sleep well at night, it is time to reduce your workload a little.

Here's how you can do that

- Always leave your office when your work hours end; yes, get up and leave. If those you work with ask you to stay back for some time, politely refuse unless there is an emergency. If your boss nags you to work long hours without your consent, report this behaviour to HR.

- If you work from home, set fixed working hours and don't work past them. You can also designate a room or a corner of your house as your workstation. This way, you will peacefully exit the spot right when your work hours end.

- Analyse your current workload, and take up only as much work as you can handle. When taking up new projects, consider your working pace, style, nature of job, temperament, and ability to handle stress. If you easily become overwhelmed, it is best to take a new project only when you have finished the previous one, that way you don't compromise quality between your projects.

- If your job is such that you have to complete specific deliverables every week, start managing your time efficiently. Work on high-priority tasks first and then cater to the seemingly low-priority ones. If you feel your boss is burdening you with extra work, talk to them and if nothing changes, report the issue to HR.

- If a certain project does not align with your interests, skillset, and goals, finish it up and don't take similar projects. If you can leave it midway, do so. Sometimes burdensome tasks get on our nerves, overwhelming us with stress and anxiety. In such cases, it is best to leave or stop taking such projects solely because they may be bringing in some extra cash, but at the cost of your happiness, this trade-off does not match.

- Stop bringing your office work home. Once you're home, you should prioritise yourself and take time to unwind and relax. If it helps, you can put up signs, or wall-art pieces that say, "Relax, Refresh, Recharge", "Take Time For Yourself", or something similar to give yourself gentle and entertaining reminders to relax once you're home.

Start respecting yourself, caring for yourself and reducing your workload to take the first step in right direction. The more cared for you feel, the less you overthink.

8: Create a worry period

For some people, it can be challenging, if not downright difficult, to give up overthinking altogether. If you're such a person, weaning yourself off from worrying comes in handy. Create a personal worry period of about 10 to 20 minutes and use this time to think about your worries. Whenever you have a perturbing concern during the day, ward it off by writing it down and reminding yourself that you will worry about it during your worry window.

Often, the worries naturally diminish by the time the worry period approaches. For concerns that persist, you have that time to think about them, ensuring they don't rattle in your head much during the day.

- Start by creating a 20 minute worry period.

- Every time a thought disturbs you during the day, take deep breaths to re-center yourself and focus on the present moment.

- Write the thought down, and tell yourself that you'll think about it later in the day during the period you set.

- Address all your concerns during this dedicated time.

- Slowly and gradually reduce your worry period from 20 to 18 to 15 minutes, and keep shortening it until it's 5 to 8 minutes long.

- During your worry period, you can think about whatever is bothering you, but instead of concerning yourself with the problem, focus on finding solutions. To do that, you have to consciously encourage yourself to think about ways to handle the situation. Ask yourself pragmatic questions such as, "How can I handle this problem?", "What can I do to improve my productivity?" or "How can I improve my relationship with my partner?". Self-questioning is one of the best ways to focus more on identifying solutions and less on problems.

As your worry period gets smaller, so do your worries, and soon, you become worry-free, which is one of the most potent antidotes against overthinking.

Action step

The journey to a happy life may seem tough right now, but it will become quite easy once you involve yourself in it and take baby steps daily. You can do it, and you will soon reach the point where you can reclaim your life for good.

You've Made It

A life marked by happiness is the one you deserve to live. It awaits your touch. Make that happen for good with this book as your constant guide by your side.

To recap:

This book has provided you with detailed and actionable information on what you can do to overcome overthinking and adopt healthy, life-changing, self-growth habits. The ball is now in your court.

Remember

You can cancel all the pointless noise in your life.

You can mute the incessant, unhappy internal chatter.

You can most certainly turn your inner voice into a positive and happy one.

 You have this power locked inside you.

All you need to do is believe in yourself, because belief is the most powerful of all emotions. The instant you believe in your power to turn things around for the better and overcome your overthinking habit, you would have achieved 50% of your goal.

To achieve the remaining 50%, you have to start taking steps towards your goals. You have all the guidelines right here in front of you. Affirm positive things to yourself, tell yourself you can accomplish your goal, and carry out the exercises taught in this book.

It can feel a bit overwhelming at first, but trust me; you have the power to do so. Deep inside, you believe that. Hold on to that belief and use it to fuel your motivation. There is light inside you; tap into it and make yourself shine!

Printed in Great Britain
by Amazon

19911674R00090